Praise

Five Moral Pieces

"The spirit of enlightenment breathes through the writings of Umberto Eco.... [He] is an urbane, genial writer who brings calmness and clarity to every subject he treats." —*Los Angeles Times*

"This little book of scarcely more than 100 pages offers challenging, and so nourishing, reading."
—*The Washington Times*

"The author of three best-selling, ingeniously plotted novels and several collections of sharp and witty essays (most recently *Kant and the Platypus*), Eco here presents five pieces on the fragility of ethical principles in postmodern culture.... In its entirety, this slim volume is cogently argued and periodically sparkles with the kind of wit and insight that readers have come to expect from one of Italy's brightest minds." —*Library Journal*

"Here Eco tackles difficult subjects with apparent ease in essays that, dealing with morality and ethics, touch every area of modern thought.... Eco combines reflections on our shared history and his recommendations for a more favorable modernity in a manner that seems indisputable and brilliant."

—*Booklist*

"Famous for his complex, erudite novels, semiotician and literary theorist Eco... devotes these occasional essays primarily to the quest for tolerance in an intolerant world and to the intellectual responsibility of individuals to confront difficult moral problems directly." —*Publishers Weekly*

"*Five Moral Pieces* packs a philosophical wallop surprising in such a slender book.... Eco's prose here is beautiful in its simplicity." —*January Magazine*

PRAISE FOR PREVIOUS COLLECTIONS OF ESSAYS BY UMBERTO ECO

Kant and the Platypus

"Puzzling, provocative, humorous, and surprisingly profound... The author is a writer of grace and wit." —*The New York Times*

"Eco's double life as a theorist of communication and a practitioner of fiction makes him exceptionally well suited to entertain and inform.... Eco is a master of saying what it is we can, with confidence, say, and he says it wonderfully."
—*San Francisco Chronicle*

"Eco's ability to balance technical subject matter with broadly intelligible anecdotes and illustrations should make it valuable and pleasurable for anyone." —*Publishers Weekly*

"What the general reader will find here is an extraordinary mind at play."
—*Sunday Times* (London)

Travels in Hyperreality

"Mr. Eco combines scholarship with a love of paradox and a quirky, sometimes outrageous, sense of humor." —*The Atlantic Monthly*

"*Travels in Hyperreality* offers a . . . scintillating collection of writings by one of the most influential thinkers of our time." —*Los Angeles Times*

"Something between, say, the boogie and boogaloo of Tom Wolfe and the stately, classic downwind sailing of John Updike."
—*The New York Times Book Review*

Serendipities

"Examines with wit and elegance some of the many cases in which a mistaken belief has led to a sound result. . . . Readers who enjoy this author's grace of style and mastery of odd anecdotes will find his reflections delightful." —*The Atlantic Monthly*

"A highly palatable, eclectic distillation of the power of language . . . Eco's genius is that he is as nimble with small details as he is with overarching concepts."
—*Publishers Weekly*

"Eco's medieval erudition gives him a magisterial perspective on contemporary culture. . . . The book, in its characteristic liveliness and good humor, will not disappoint fans of the professor."
—*The Toronto Star*

Five Moral Pieces

Also by Umberto Eco

Baudolino

Kant and the Platypus

Semiotics and the Philosophy of Language

A Theory of Semiotics

Serendipities

How to Travel with a Salmon

Misreadings

Travels in Hyperreality

The Island of the Day Before

Foucault's Pendulum

Postscript to The Name of the Rose

The Name of the Rose

Umberto Eco

Five Moral Pieces

TRANSLATED FROM THE ITALIAN
BY ALASTAIR MCEWEN

A HARVEST BOOK
HARCOURT, INC.
SAN DIEGO NEW YORK LONDON

www.HarcourtBooks.com

This is a translation of *Cinque Scritti Morali*

Library of Congress Cataloging-in-Publication Data
Eco, Umberto.
[Cinque scritti morali. English]
Five moral pieces/Umberto Eco; translated from the Italian by Alastair McEwen.—1st U.S. ed.
p. cm.
ISBN 0-15-100446-3
ISBN 0-15-601325-8 (pbk.)
I. Title.
PQ4865.C6 C5613 2001
854'.914—dc21 2001024312

Text set in Stempel Garamond
Designed by Linda Lockowitz

Printed in the United States of America

First Harvest edition 2002
C E G I K J H F D B

Contents

Introduction

The essays collected here have two things in common. They are, first, occasional pieces: pieces that sprang from talks given at conferences, articles on current affairs. And, despite the variety of their themes, they are all ethical in nature, that is to say, they treat of what we ought to do, what we ought not to do, and what we must not do at any cost.

Given their occasional nature, I should explain the circumstances in which they were written.

"Reflections on War" was published in *La Rivista dei libri,* 1 April 1991, at the time of the Gulf War.

"When the Other Appears on the Scene" is derived from an exchange of four letters with Cardinal Martini organized and published by *Liberal* magazine. The correspondence was then brought together in a slim volume, *Che cosa crede chi non crede?* (Rome: Atlantide Editoriale, 1996). My text is a reply to a question the cardinal had put to me: "What is the basis of the certainty and necessity for moral action of those who, in order to establish the absolute nature of an ethic, do not intend to appeal to *metaphysical principles* or transcendental values, or even to universally valid *categorical imperatives?*" For the background to the debate the reader is referred to the volume in question, which also contains notes and contributions by Emanuele Severino, Manlio Sgalambro, Eugenio Scalfari, Indro Montanelli, Vittorio Foa, and Claudio Martelli.

"On the Press" was a paper presented in the course of a series of seminars organized by the Italian Senate (President Carlo Scognamiglio), before the members of the Senate and the editors of Italy's biggest dailies, with whom a wide-ranging discussion then followed. The text was subsequently published, by the Senate itself, in *Gli Incontri di studio a Palazzo Giustiniani: Stampa e mondo politico oggi* (Rome: Tipografia del Senato, 1995), a volume that also contains the addresses given by Scognamiglio, Eugenio Scalfari, Giulio Anselmi, Francesco Tabladini, Silvano Boroli, Walter Veltroni, Salvatore Carruba, Darko Bratina, Livio Caputo, and Paolo Mieli.

"Ur-Fascism" was a speech given in English at a symposium organized by the Italian and French departments of Columbia University, on 25 April 1995, in commemoration of the Liberation of Europe. It later appeared as "Ur-Fascism" in *The New York Review of Books* (22 June 1995) and was translated into Italian for the June-July 1995 number of *La Rivista dei libri* with the title "Totalitarismo *fuzzy* e Ur-Fascismo" (a version virtually the same as the one published here except for a few minor modifications). However, it should be borne in mind that the text was conceived for an audience of American students and the speech was given in the days when America was still shaken by outrage over the Oklahoma city bombing and by the discovery of the fact (by no means a secret) that extreme right-wing military organizations existed in America. The anti-Fascist theme, therefore, took on particular connotations in that context, and my historical observations were intended to stimulate reflection on current problems in various countries—the talk was then translated by newspapers and magazines into numerous other languages. Furthermore, the fact that the discourse was aimed at young Americans explains the presence of specific information on events that an Italian reader ought to know about already, such as the quotations from Roosevelt, the allusions to American anti-Fascism, and the emphasis on the encounter between Europeans and Americans at the time of the Liberation.

"Migration, Tolerance, and the Intolerable" is a collage. The first section contains the first part of a talk given on 23 January 1997 on the opening of the conference organized by the city of Valencia regarding prospects for the third millennium. The second is a translation and readaptation of the introduction to the International Forum on Intolerance, organized in Paris by the Académie Universelle des Cultures on 26 and 27 March 1997. The third, titled "Non chiediamoci per chi suona la campana," was published by *La Repubblica* on the occasion of the sentencing of former SS officer Erich Priebke, accused of war crimes and tried before the Rome Military Tribunal.

Reflections on War

This article considers War with a capital W, as in "hot" war waged with the explicit consensus of nations, in the form it has assumed in the contemporary world. Since I will be submitting this piece just as Allied troops enter Kuwait City, it is probable—provided there are no surprises—that when people read it they will all feel that the Gulf War has led to a satisfactory outcome, because it is in conformity with the goals for which it was begun. In this case any talk of the impossibility or uselessness of war would seem like a contradiction: no one would be prepared to maintain that an undertaking that leads to a desired result is either useless or impossible. Yet the following reflections *must* hold no matter how things turn out. Indeed, they must hold a fortiori were the war to make it possible to attain "advantageous" results, precisely because this would convince everyone that war is still, in certain cases, a reasonable alternative. While one is always duty-bound to deny this.

Since the war began, we have heard or read various appeals criticizing "intellectuals" for not having adopted the proper stance with regard to this tragedy. Since the vocal majority that says or writes things like this is usually represented by intellectuals (in the strict sense of the term), one wonders about the makeup of the silent minority from whom a statement is required. Clearly the minority is composed of those who did not give a "correct" opinion on the matter when the time came to choose sides. Proof of this lies in the fact that, day after day, if someone puts forth an opinion contrary to the expectations of someone else, he or she is promptly labeled an intellectual traitor, a capitalist warmonger or a pro-Arab pacifist. The clash within the vocal majority as it emerged through the mass media ensured that each party deserved the other's accusations. Supporters of the ineluctable necessity of the conflict appeared to be interventionists of the old school; the pacifists, largely incapable of eschewing the slogans and rituals of past decades, unfailingly deserved to be accused of wishing for the surrender of one side in order to reward the belligerence of the other. In a form of ritual exorcism, those who supported the conflict were obliged to begin by stating how cruel war is, while those who were against it had to begin by stating how cruel Saddam is.

In each of these cases we have certainly witnessed a debate between professional intellectuals, but what we have not seen is the practice of the intellectual function. As we all know, intellectuals are a very nebulous thing as a category. But defining the "intellectual function" is a different matter. It consists of identifying critically what one considers a satisfactory approximation of one's own concept of truth—and this can be done by anybody, even by social misfits who reflect on their own condition and express it in some way, while it may be betrayed by writers who react emotionally to events, without subjecting themselves to the purification of thought.

This is why, as Vittorini put it, intellectuals must not "play the piper to revolution." Not in order to shirk the responsibility of a choice (which they can make as individuals), but because the moment of action requires the elimination of nuances and ambiguities (and this is the irreplaceable function of the "decision maker" in every institution), whereas the intellectual function lies in delving for ambiguities and bringing them to light. The first duty of the intellectual is to criticize his own traveling companions ("to think" means to play the voice of conscience). It may happen that the intellectual opts to keep silent because he fears betraying those with whom he identifies, thinking that, despite their contingent errors, their goal is basically the maximum good for all.

A tragic decision, of which the history books are full, and for which some have gone to their death, in a struggle in which they did not believe, because they thought they could not trade loyalty for truth. But loyalty is a moral category, while the truth is a theoretical one.

It is not that the intellectual function is detached from morality. It is a moral decision when we put it into practice, just as it is a moral decision that prompts the surgeon to cut into living flesh in order to save a life. But when the time comes to cut, the surgeon must not yield to emotion, not even when he or she decides to close the incision because it is not worth carrying on with the operation. The intellectual function can also lead to emotionally unbearable results, *because at times some problems must be solved by demonstrating that they cannot be solved.* It is a moral decision to express one's own conclusion—or to remain silent about it (perhaps in the hope that it is mistaken). Such is the drama of those who, even momentarily, take on the task of playing the "representatives of mankind."

Many have waxed ironical, even in the Catholic world, about the position of the pope, who has said that we must not make war, who has prayed, and proposed solutions that seemed negligible in comparison with the complexity of events. In order to justify him, friends and enemies have concluded that the poor man was only doing his job, because he could hardly have said otherwise. This is right. The pope (from his own standpoint about the truth) exercised his intellectual function and said that we must not make war. The pope is obliged to say that, if we wish to follow the Gospels to the letter, we must turn the other cheek. But what am I to do if someone wants to kill me? "That's your lookout," the pope *ought* to say, "your problem"—and casuistry on self-defense would then come into play only with a view to making up for human frailties, which no one ought to feel obliged to provide a heroic defense of. The position is so impeccable that if (and when) the pope adds something else that can be understood as a practical suggestion, he abandons his own intellectual function and makes political decisions (and that's *his* problem).

If this is the case, it needs to be said that for the last forty-five years the intellectual community has not been silent on the problem of war. It has talked about it, and with such missionary commitment that the world's view of war has been radically modified. Never as on this occasion have people felt all the horror and ambiguity of what was happening. Apart from a few lunatics, no one had ideas in black and white. The fact that the war broke out all the same is a sign that the intellectuals' discourse has not been an unqualified success. It has not been sufficient, and has not been granted sufficient attention historically. But this is an accident. The modern world looks at war through eyes different from those with which it looked at the problem early in the twentieth century, and if someone were to talk today of the beauty of war as the only form of world hygiene, he would go down not in the annals of literature but in those of psychiatry. What has happened to war is what has happened to crimes of passion or the *lex talionis*: people still do these things, but the community now considers them to be evil, whereas it once judged them to be a good thing.

But these would still be moral and emotional reactions (and at times ethics itself can accept exceptions to the prohibition on killing, just as the collective sensibility can accept horrors and sacrifices that guarantee a greater good). There is a more radical way of thinking about war: in merely formal terms, in terms of internal consistency, by reflecting on its conditions of possibility—the conclusion being that you cannot make war because the existence of a society based on instant information, rapid transport, and continuous intercontinental migration, allied to the nature of the new technologies of war, has made war impossible and irrational. War is in contradiction with the very reasons for which it is waged.

Over the centuries, what has been the purpose of warfare? War was waged to defeat an adversary, in order to benefit from his defeat, and in such a way that our intentions—to act in a certain manner, to attain a certain result—were tactically or strategically conceived with a view to making our adversary's intentions impracticable. To these ends it was necessary to field all the forces at our disposal. At the end of the day, the game was played out between us and our adversary. The neutrality of the others, the fact that our war did not bother them (and that to a certain extent it allowed them to profit from it), was a necessary condition for our freedom to maneuver. Not even Clausewitz's "total war" could escape these restrictions.

It is only in our century that the notion of "world war" was born, in other words a war capable of involving even societies without a history, like Polynesian tribal societies. The discovery of atomic energy, television, air transport, and the birth of various forms of multinational capitalism have resulted in some conditions that make war impossible.

1. Nuclear weapons have persuaded everybody that an atomic conflict would produce no winners and a sole loser—the planet. But after the realization dawned that atomic war is antiecological, the conviction grew that all wars are antiecological and cannot be otherwise. Anyone destroying forests with substances like Agent Orange (or polluting the sea) declares war not only on neutral powers but on the earth as a whole.

2. War is no longer waged on a front between two sides. The scandal of the American journalists in Baghdad is the same as the scandal, of far greater dimensions, of millions and millions of pro-Iraqi Muslims who live in the countries of the

anti-Iraqi coalition. In the wars of the past, potential enemies were interned (or massacred), while compatriots who spoke in favor of the enemy's cause from enemy territory were usually hanged as soon as the war was over. But war can no longer be frontal, because of the very nature of multinational capitalism. That Iraq was armed by western industry is no accident. It falls within the logic of mature capitalism, which eludes the control of individual states. When the American government finds that the television companies are playing the enemy's game, it still thinks it is faced with a plot hatched by pro-Communist eggheads. In the same way, the television companies labor under the illusion that they are the impersonation of Humphrey Bogart, who has the corrupt gangster listen to the sound of the printing presses over the telephone as he says: "It's the press, old chum, and you can't stop it." But the logic of the news industry demands that it sell news, preferably dramatic news. It is not that the media refuse to play along with war: the media are merely a pianola performing a piece previously transcribed on its roll. In modern wars, therefore, everyone has the enemy behind the lines, something Clausewitz never could have accepted.

3. Even when the media are gagged, the new technologies of communication permit an unstop-

pable flow of information—and not even a dictator can prevent this, because such technologies make use of fundamental infrastructures that he cannot do without either. This flow of information assumes the role played in traditional wars by the secret services: it neutralizes every surprise action—and you cannot have a war in which it is impossible to surprise the enemy. War produces a general exchange of intelligence with the enemy. But information does more: it continually allows the enemy to speak (while the aim of all wartime policy is to block enemy propaganda), and demoralizes the citizens of the contending parties with regard to their own government (while Clausewitz points out that a condition for victory is the moral cohesion of the combatant). Every war of the past was based on the principle that the citizens, believing it to be a just war, were anxious to destroy the enemy. Now information not only shakes the faith of the citizens, it also leaves them vulnerable when faced with the death of the enemy—no longer a distant and vague event but instead unbearable visual evidence.

4. All this interacts with the fact that, as Foucault put it, power is no longer monolithic and monocephalous: it is diffused, packeted, made of the continuous agglomeration and breaking down of consensus. War no longer pits two native

lands one against the other. It puts a multiplicity of powers into competition with one another. In this game individual centers of power gain an advantage, but at the expense of the others. Whereas traditional war made fortunes for arms merchants, and this gain reduced the importance of the temporary suspension of some kinds of commerce, the new warfare, while it still enriches arms merchants, triggers a worldwide crisis for industries like air transport, entertainment and tourism, the media themselves (which lose out on advertising revenues), and the entire industry of the superfluous in general—the backbone of the system—from the construction market to car manufacturing. When news breaks of a war in progress, the stock market bounds upward, but one month later the same market makes a similar leap when the first signs of a possible peace begin to emerge. No "cynicism" in the first case, and no virtue in the second. The stock market records the oscillations in the play of powers. In war some economic powers find themselves in competition with others, and the logic of their conflict overwhelms that of national powers. While the industry of state consumption (such as armaments) needs tension, that of individual consumption needs happiness. The clash is played out in economic terms.

5. For all these and other reasons war no longer resembles, like the wars of the old days, a "serial" intelligent system, but rather a "parallel" intelligent system. A serial intelligent system, used for example to build machines capable of translating or drawing inferences from some given information, is instructed by the programmer so that it can make, on the basis of a finite number of rules, subsequent decisions, each of which depends on an assessment of the preceding decision, in accordance with a tree structure, made of a series of binary disjunctions. Old-fashioned military strategies went like this: if the enemy has moved his troops to the east, then perhaps he intends to proceed southward; I shall therefore move my troops in a northeasterly direction, to bar his way in a surprise move. The enemy's rules were our rules too, and each party made one decision at a time, as in a game of chess.

   A parallel system, on the other hand, requires the individual cells of a network to assume a final configuration in accordance with a pattern of weights that the programmer cannot decide on or foresee beforehand, because the network finds rules that have not been received previously, modifies itself accordingly, and cannot distinguish between rules and data. True, a system of this kind (called a "neoconnectionist" or "neural network" system) can be controlled by comparing the given response with the expected response and adjusting the weights through successive experiments. But this requires (1) that the operator has the time, (2) that there are not two competing operators who redistribute the weights in a reciprocally contradictory fashion, and finally (3) that the individual cells of the network "think" as cells and not as operators—i.e., that they do not act on the basis of inferences made about the behavior of the operators, and above all that they do not have interests extraneous to the logic of the network itself. In a system in which power is packeted, every cell acts in accordance with its own interests, which are not those of the operator and have nothing to do with the autodynamic tendencies of the network. Consequently, if—albeit only metaphorically—war is a neoconnectionist system, it takes a path that is independent of the will of the two parties in contention. It is interesting how, in explaining the workings of a neural network, Arno Penzias (in *Come vivere in un mondo High-Tech,* Milano: Bompiani, 1989, pp. 107–08) uses a military metaphor:

It was known that individual neurons became electrically active ('they fired') if stimulated by their finely ramified input cables (called *den-*

> *drites*). When it 'fires', a neuron emits electrical signals along a series of output cables (called *axons*) . . . Since the 'firing' of each neuron depends on the activity of many others, there is no simple way of calculating what should happen or when. [. . .] According to the particular disposition of the synaptic connections, every simulation of a network of a hundred neurons defined its own set of possible states of equilibrium (out of a total of absolute possibilities of one thousand billion billion billions, or 10^{30}).

If war is a neoconnectionist system, it is no longer a phenomenon in which the calculations and intentions of the protagonists have any value. Owing to the multiplication of the powers in play, war distributes itself according to unpredictable patterns of weights. It may resolve itself in a way that is convenient for one of the opposing parties; but in principle, since it defies all decisional calculations, it is lost for both parties. The operators' frenetic attempts to control the network, which receives contradictory impulses, will cause it to collapse. The most likely outcome of a war is "tilt." Old-fashioned wars were like a game of chess in which each player could try to take as many of his opponent's pieces as possible, but the ultimate goal was checkmate. Instead, contemporary warfare is like a chess game in which both players (working on the same network) move and take pieces of the same color. Modern warfare is therefore an autophagous game.

To state that a conflict has turned out to be advantageous for someone at a given moment implies an equation of that momentary advantage with the final advantage. There would be a final moment if war were still, as Clausewitz would have it, the continuation of policy by other means (hence the war would end when the situation reached a state of equilibrium sufficient to permit a return to politics). But in our century it is the politics of the postwar period that will always be the continuation (by any means) of the premises established by war. No matter how the war goes, by causing a general redistribution of weights that cannot correspond fully with the will of the contending parties, it will drag on in the form of a dramatic political, economic, and psychological instability for decades to come, something that can lead only to a politics "waged" as if it were warfare.

Have things ever been any different? Is it forbidden to think that Clausewitz was wrong? Historiography has reinterpreted Waterloo as a clash between two intelligences (because there was a result), but Stendhal interpreted it in terms of accident. To conclude that classic wars produced reasonable results—a final equilibrium—derives from a Hegelian prejudice, according to which history has a positive direction. There is no scientific (or logical) proof that the order of the Mediterranean after the

Punic Wars, or that of Europe after the Napoleonic Wars, corresponded perforce with a state of equilibrium. It could have been a state of imbalance that would not have occurred had there been no war. The fact that for tens of thousands of years humanity has used warfare as a solution for states of disequilibrium has no more demonstrable value than the fact that in the same period humanity learned to resolve states of psychological imbalance by using alcohol or other equally devastating substances.

And this brings us to the notion of taboos. Moravia suggested that, since it took centuries for humanity to develop the incest taboo because of the realization that endogamy gave negative results, we have perhaps reached the point in which humanity has become aware of the need to proclaim war a taboo. Realists have replied that a taboo is not "proclaimed" by moral or intellectual decree, it is formed over millennia in the obscure recesses of the collective consciousness (just as a neural network, in the end, can attain a state of equilibrium on its own). Of course, a taboo is not proclaimed: it proclaims itself. But the times required for growth are shortening. Becoming aware that mating with mothers or sisters hindered exchange between groups took thousands of years—it apparently took humanity ages to grasp the cause-and-effect relation between the sexual act and pregnancy. But it took us only two weeks to realize that airline companies close when war breaks out. It is therefore compatible with intellectual duty and with common sense to announce the necessity for a taboo, although no one has the authority to say that a certain time is required for its coming to maturity.

It is an intellectual duty to proclaim the inconceivability of war. Even if there were no alternative solutions. At most, to remind people that our century has known an *excellent* alternative to war, and that is "cold" war. In the end, history will have to admit that cold warfare, the source of horrors, injustices, intolerance, local conflicts, and widespread terror, has proved a very humane and mild solution in terms of casualties, and cold warfare can even boast victors and vanquished. But declaring cold wars is not a task for the intellectual.

What struck some as the silence of intellectuals about war was perhaps their fear of talking about it in the media in the heat of the moment, and this for the simple reason that the media are a part of war and its paraphernalia, and so it is dangerous to think of the media as neutral territory. Above all, the media work on a different time scale. The intellectual function is always exercised ahead of time (regarding what might happen) or with hindsight (regarding what has happened), seldom with regard to what is actually happening, for reasons of rhythm, because events are always faster and more relentless than reflection on events can be. This is why Calvino's Baron Cosimo Piovasco di Rondò stayed up in his tree: not to shirk the intellectual duty to understand and to take part in his day and age, but to be able to understand and take part in it better.

However, even when it opts for tactical silence, in the end reflection on war requires that this silence must eventually be articulated. In complete awareness of the contradictions of a proclamation of silence, of the persuasive power of an act of impotence, and of the fact that the exercise of reflection exempts no one from the assumption of individual responsibility. But our first duty is to say that war today annuls all human initiative, and even its apparent purpose (and someone's apparent victory) cannot stop what has become the autonomous game of *weights* caught in their own net.

War cannot be justified, because—in terms of the rights of the species—it is worse than a crime. It is a waste.

When the Other Appears on the Scene

Dear Carlo Maria Martini,

Your letter has extricated me from one serious dilemma only to leave me on the horns of another that is equally awkward. Until now it has been up to me (through no decision of mine) to open the debate, and he who talks first inevitably puts his questions and invites the other to reply. My predicament springs from my feeling inquisitorial. And I very much appreciated the firmness and humility with which you, on three occasions, exploded the myth that would have us believe that Jesuits always answer a question with another question.

But now I am at a loss as to how to reply to your question, because my answer would be significant had I had a lay upbringing. But in fact I received a strongly Catholic education until (just to record the moment of the breach) the age of twenty-two. For me, the lay point of view was not a passively absorbed heritage, but rather the hard-won result of a long and slow process of change, and I always wonder whether some of my moral convictions do not still depend on religious impressions received early in my development. Now, in my maturity, I have seen (in a foreign Catholic university that also employs lay teaching staff, requiring of them no more than a manifestation of formal respect during religious-academic rituals) some of my colleagues take the sacraments without their believing in the Real Presence, and therefore without their having taken confession beforehand. With a tremor, after so many years, I felt once more the horror of sacrilege.

Nonetheless, I feel I can explain the foundations on which my "lay religiosity" rests—because I firmly hold that there are forms of religiosity, and therefore a sense of the Holy, of the Limit, of questioning and of awaiting, of communion with something that transcends us, even in the absence of faith in a personal and provident divinity. But, as I see from your letter, you know this too. What you are asking yourself is what is binding, captivating, and inalienable in these forms of ethic.

I should like to approach things in a roundabout way. Certain ethical problems became clearer to me on considering some problems in semantics—and please don't worry if some people say that we are talking in a complicated way: they might have been encouraged to think too simply by mass-media "revelations," predictable by definition. Let them instead learn to "think complicated," because neither the mystery nor the evidence is simple.

My problem hinged on the existence of "semantic universals," or in other words, elementary notions that are common to the entire human species and can be expressed in all languages. Not such an easy problem, given that many cultures do not recognize notions that strike us as obvious: for example, that of substance to which certain properties belong (as when we say that "the apple is red") or that of identity ($a = a$). However, I am convinced that there certainly are notions common to all cultures, and that they all refer to the position of our body in space.

We are erect animals, so it is tiring to stay upside down for long, and therefore we have a common notion of up and down, tending to favor the first over the second. Likewise, we have notions of right and left, of standing still and of walking, of standing up and lying down, of crawling and jumping, of waking and sleeping. Since we have limbs, we all know what it means to beat against a resistant material, to penetrate a soft or liquid substance, to crush, to drum, to pummel, to kick, and perhaps even to dance as well. The list is a long one, and could include seeing, hearing, eating or drinking, swallowing or excreting. And certainly every human being has notions about the meaning of perceiving, recalling, feeling desire, fear, sorrow, relief, pleasure or pain, and of emitting sounds that express these things. Therefore (and we are already in the sphere of rights) there are universal concepts regarding constriction: we do not want anyone to prevent us from talking, seeing, listening, sleeping, swallowing, or excreting, or from going where we wish; we suffer if someone binds or segregates us, beats, wounds, or kills us, or subjects us to physical or psychological torture that diminishes or annuls our capacity to think.

Note that until now I have described only a sort of bestial and solitary Adam, who still knows nothing of sexual relations, the pleasures of dialogue, love for his offspring, or the pain of losing a loved one; but already in this phase, at least for *us* (if not for him or for her) this semantics has become the basis of an ethic: first and foremost we must respect the rights of the corporeality of others, which also include the right to talk and think. If our fellows had respected these "rights of the body," we would never have had the Slaughter of the Innocents, the Christians in the circus, Saint Bartholomew's Night, the burning of heretics, the death camps, censorship, child labor in mines, or the rapes in Bosnia.

But how is it that this marveling and ferocious beast that I have described immediately works out his (or her) instinctive repertoire of universal notions and can reach the point where he understands not only that he wishes to do certain things and does not wish other things to be done to him, but also that he should not do to others what he does not wish to be done to him? Because, luckily, Eden is soon populated. The ethical dimension begins when the other appears on the scene. Every law, moral or juridical as it may be, regulates interpersonal relationships, including those with an other who imposes that law.

You too say that virtuous laypersons are persuaded that the other is within us. However, this is not a vague emotional inclination but a fundamental condition. As we are taught by the most secular of the human sciences, it is the other, it is his look, that defines and forms us. Just as we cannot live without eating or sleeping, we cannot understand who we are without the look and the response of the other. Even those who kill, rape, rob, or oppress do this in exceptional moments, but they spend the rest of their lives soliciting from their fellows approval, love, respect, and praise. And even from those they humiliate they ask the recognition of fear and submission. In the absence of this recognition, the newborn baby abandoned in the forest does not become humanized (or like Tarzan seeks at all costs the other in the face of an ape), and the result of living in a community in which everyone had decided systematically never to look at us, treating us as if we did not exist, would be madness or death.

Why is it then that there are or have been cultures that approve of massacre, cannibalism, or the humiliation of the bodies of others? Simply because such cultures restrict the concept of "others" to the tribal community (or the ethnic group) and consider "barbarians" to be nonhumans; but not even the Crusaders felt that unbelievers were fellowmen worthy of an excessive degree of love. The fact is that the recognition of the roles of others, the necessity to respect in them those requirements we consider essential for ourselves, is the product of thousands of years of development. Even the Christian commandment to love was enunciated, and laboriously accepted, only when the time was ripe.

But you ask me: Is this awareness of the importance of the other sufficient to provide us with an absolute basis, an immutable foundation for ethical behavior? It would suffice for me to reply that even those things that you define as "absolute foundations" do not prevent many believers from knowingly sinning, and there the matter would end. The temptation of evil is present even in those who possess a well-founded and revealed notion of good. But I want to tell you two anecdotes, which gave me much to think about.

One concerns a writer, who describes himself as a Catholic, albeit of the sui generis variety, whose name I shall not give only because he told me what I am about to quote in the course of a private conversation, and I am not a talebearer. It was in the days of the papacy of John XXIII, and my elderly friend, in enthusiastically praising the pope's virtues, said (with clearly paradoxical intentions): "Pope John must be an atheist. Only a man who does not believe in God can love his fellowman so much!" Like all paradoxes, this one also contains a grain of truth: without troubling to consider the atheist (a type whose psychology eludes me, because, as Kant observed, I do not see how one can *not* believe in God, and hold that His existence can *not* be proved, and then firmly believe in the nonexistence of God, holding that this *can* be proved), it seems clear to me that a person who has never had any experience of the transcendent, or who has lost it, can make sense of his or her life and death, can be comforted by love for others, and by the attempt to guarantee someone else a life to be lived even after his or her own death. Of course, there are people who do not believe and nonetheless do not trouble to make sense of their own death, but there are also those who say they believe but who would be prepared to rip the heart out of a child in order to ward off death. The strength of an ethic is judged on the behavior of saints, not on the foolish *cujus deus venter est.*

This brings me to the second anecdote. I was still a sixteen-year-old Catholic boy when I happened to cross swords in a verbal duel with an older acquaintance who was a known "communist," in the sense in which the term was employed in the terrible fifties. And since he was provoking me, I asked him the decisive question: how could he, as a nonbeliever, make sense of that otherwise senseless event that was his own death? And he replied: "By asking before dying that I might have a civil funeral. And so I am no more, but I have set an example for others." I think that you too can admire the profound faith in the continuity of life, the absolute sense of duty that inspired his reply. And it is this sentiment that has induced many nonbelievers to die under torture rather than betray their friends, and others to catch the plague in order to look after plague victims. And sometimes it is also the only thing that drives a philosopher to philosophize, and a writer to write: to leave a message in the bottle, because in some way what we believe in, or what we think is beautiful, might be believed in or found beautiful by posterity.

Is this feeling really strong enough to justify an ethic as determined and inflexible, as solidly established as the ethic of those who believe in revealed morality, in the survival of the soul, in reward and punishment? I have tried to base the principles of a lay ethics on a natural reality (and, as such, in your view too, the result of a divine plan) like our corporeality and the idea that we instinctively know that we have a soul (or something that serves as such) only by virtue of the presence of others. It would appear that what I have defined as a "lay ethics" is at bottom a natural ethics, which not even believers deny. Is not the natural instinct, brought to the right level of maturity and self-awareness, a foundation offering sufficient guarantees? Of course we may think this an insufficient spur to virtue. "In any case," nonbelievers can say, "no one will know of the evil I am secretly doing." But those who do not believe think that no one is watching them from on high, and therefore they also know that—precisely for this reason—there is not even a Someone who may forgive. If such people know they have done ill, their solitude shall be without end, and their death desperate. They will opt, more than believers, for the purification of public confession, they will ask the forgiveness of others. This they know, in the deepest part of their being, and therefore they know that they should forgive others first. Otherwise how could we explain that *remorse* is a feeling known to nonbelievers too?

I should not like to establish a clear-cut opposition between those who believe in a transcendent God and those who believe in no superindividual principle. I should like to point out that it was precisely ethics that inspired the title of Spinoza's great work, which begins with a definition of God as the cause of Himself. But Spinoza's divinity, as we well know, is neither transcendent nor personal: yet even the vision of a great and single cosmic *substance* in which one day we shall be reabsorbed can reveal a vision of tolerance and benevolence precisely because we are all interested in the equilibrium and harmony of this sole *substance.* This is so because we tend to think it impossible for this *substance* not to be in some way enhanced or deformed by the things we have done over the millennia. Thus I would also dare say (this is not a metaphysical hypothesis, it is merely a timid concession to the hope that never abandons us) that even from such a standpoint we could table the problem of some kind of life after death. Today the electronic universe suggests that sequences of messages can be transferred from one physical medium to another without losing their unique characteristics, and it seems that they can exist even as pure immaterial algorithms when, one medium having been abandoned, they are not transcribed again onto another. And who knows whether death, rather than an implosion, is not an explosion and the impressing, somewhere, among the vortices of the universe, of the software (which others call "soul") we have developed in life, made up of memories and personal remorse, and therefore of incurable suffering, or of a sense of peace for duty done, and love.

But you say that, without the example and the word of Christ, all lay ethics would lack a basic justification imbued with an ineluctable power of conviction. Why deprive laypersons of the right to avail themselves of the example of a forgiving Christ? Try, Carlo Maria Martini, for the good of the discussion and of the dialogue in which you believe, to accept even if only for a moment the idea that there is no God; that man appeared in the world out of a blunder on the part of a maladroit fate, delivered not only unto his mortal condition but also condemned to be aware of this, and for this reason the most imperfect of all creatures (if I may be permitted the echoes of Leopardi in this suggestion). This man, in order to find the courage to await death, would necessarily become a religious animal, and would aspire to the construction of narratives capable of providing him with an explanation and a model, an exemplary image. And among the many stories he imagines—some dazzling, some awe-inspiring, some pathetically comforting—in the fullness of time he has at a certain point the religious, moral, and poetic strength to conceive the model of Christ, of universal love, of forgiveness for enemies, of a life sacrificed that others may be saved. If I were a traveler from a distant galaxy and I found myself confronted with a species capable of proposing this model, I would be filled with admiration for such theogonic energy, and I would judge this wretched and vile species, which has committed so many horrors, redeemed were it only for the fact that it has managed to wish and to believe that all this is the *truth.*

You are now free to leave the hypothesis to others: but admit that even if Christ were only the subject of a great story, the fact that this story could have been imagined and desired by humans, creatures who know only that they do not know, would be just as miraculous (miraculously mysterious) as the son of a real God's being made flesh. This natural and worldly mystery would not cease to move and ennoble the hearts of those who do not believe.

This is why I believe that, on the fundamental points, a natural ethic—respected for the profound religiosity that inspires it—can find common ground with the principles of an ethic founded on faith in transcendence, which cannot fail to recognize that natural principles have been carved into our hearts on the basis of a plan for salvation. If this leaves, as it certainly does, margins that may not overlap, it is no different from what happens when different religions encounter one another. And in conflicts of faith, *charity* and *prudence* must prevail.

On the Press

Senators,

What I am about to put before you is a *cahier de doléances* on the situation of the Italian press, especially with regard to its relations with the world of politics. I can do this in the presence of representatives of the press, and not behind their backs, because I have been saying what I intend to say here since the early sixties, mostly in the pages of Italian newspapers and weeklies. This means that we are living in a country where a free and unbiased press is able to put itself on trial.

The function of the fourth estate is certainly that of keeping a check on and criticizing the other three traditional estates (together with economic power and that represented by political parties and the labor unions), but it can do this in a free country because its criticism has no repressive function. The mass media can influence the political life of the country only by creating opinion. But the traditional powers cannot control or criticize the media other than through the media itself; otherwise their intervention becomes a sanction—either executive or legislative or judiciary—which can happen only if the media commit crimes, or appear to lead to the formation of political and institutional imbalance (see the debate on the *par condicio,* or equal-access law). But since the media, and in our case the press, cannot be exempt from criticism, it is a condition of health for a democratic country that the press put itself on the stand.

Yet this alone is frequently not enough. Indeed, it can constitute a good excuse, or, more specifically, a case of what Marcuse called "repressive tolerance." Once it has demonstrated its self-flagellatory impartiality, the press no longer feels any interest in reforming itself. About twenty years ago I was asked to write a long article criticizing *Espresso* magazine, which was published by *Espresso* itself. This may be excessive modesty on my part, but if *Espresso* subsequently took a turn for the better, it was thanks not to my article but to the natural evolution of things. As far as I recall, my criticisms made no difference.

In drawing up this *cahier de doléances* of mine, I do not intend to criticize the press in its relations with the world of politics as if the world of politics were an innocent victim of the abuses of the press. I maintain that politics bears full joint responsibility for the situation that I shall try to outline here.

I am not one of those provincial types for whom things go wrong only at home. Nor will I fall victim to the error of the Italian press, whose love of things foreign is such that whenever mention is made of a non-Italian daily the name of the publication is almost always preceded by the adjective "authoritative," to the point that all foreign evening newspapers are thus described even when they are fourth-rate rags. Most of the evils that afflict the Italian press today are common in almost all countries. But I shall make negative reference to other countries only when this is strictly necessary, because "two wrongs never make a right." And I shall take examples from other countries when it seems to me that they have a positive lesson for us.

One last specification: the texts I shall refer to are *La Repubblica,* the *Corriere della Sera,* and *Espresso,* and this is out of a spirit of fair play. These are publications I have written for or still write for, so my criticisms cannot be deemed preconceived or inspired by ill will. But the problems I shall try to throw light on regard the Italian press as a whole.

The Polemics of the Sixties and Seventies

In the sixties and seventies the polemic about the nature and function of the press hinged on these two themes: (1) the difference between news and commentary, and therefore the need for objectivity; (2) newspapers are instruments of power, run by political parties or economic groups, which use a deliberately cryptic language insofar as their real function is not to give news to the citizens but to send messages in code to another power group, passing over the heads of the readers. The language of politics was inspired by the same principles and the Italian expression "parallel convergences" has remained in the literature on mass media as a symbol of this language, which is barely comprehensible in the corridors of the Italian parliament but quite incomprehensible to the man in the street.

As we shall see, these two themes are largely obsolete. On the one hand there was an enormous polemic about objectivity, and many of us maintained that (apart from a bulletin giving rainfall statistics) there is no such thing as a really objective news item. Even if commentary and news are scrupulously separated, the very choice of the news item and its paging constitutes elements of implicit judgment. In recent decades so-called topicalization has been widely employed: the same page contains news items that are in some way connected. As an example of topicalization here is page 17 of *La Repubblica* of Sunday, 22 January 1955. Four articles: "Brescia—Woman Gives Birth and Lets Daughter Die"; "Rome—Four-Year-Old Left Alone at Home Found Playing on Windowsill, Father Winds Up in Prison"; "Rome—Even Women Who Do Not Wish to Keep Their Children Can Give Birth in a Hospital"; "Treviso—Divorced Mother Resigns as Mom." As you can see, the risk of abandoned children has been topicalized. The question we have to put ourselves is: Is this a problem typical of this period? Is there news of all the cases of this type? If it were only a matter of four cases, the matter would be statistically irrelevant; but topicalization raises the news to what classical judicial and deliberative rhetoric called an *exemplum*: a single case from which we take (or are surreptitiously invited to take) a rule. If four cases are dealt with, the newspaper leads us to think there are many more; if there were many more, the paper would not have told us. Topicalization does not merely provide four news items; it expresses a strong opinion on the situation of childhood, whatever the intentions of the editor who, perhaps in the small hours, made page 17 up that way because he or she did not know how to fill it. By this I am not saying that the technique of topicalization is mistaken or dangerous. All I am saying is that it shows us how opinions can be expressed in the giving of entirely objective news items.

As for the problem of cryptic language, I would say that the Italian press has abandoned this, because changes have also occurred in the language of politicians, who no longer read out obscure and elaborate phrases from a slip of paper into the microphones, but say *apertis verbis* that their colleague is a traitor to the group, while others brag vociferously about the erectile qualities of their reproductive organ.[1] In fact the press has fallen back on a

---

[1]A reference to the leader of Italy's Northern League, Umberto Bossi, who claims that the league "*ce l'ha duro*" (literally, has a hard cock).

language within the grasp of that magmatic entity known today as "folks," but it maintains that people talk only in clichés. Here therefore (I am using snippets of data collected by my students, who spent a month checking the Italian press for clichés) is a list of clichés taken from a single article in the *Corriere della Sera* of 11 January 1995: "Hope springs eternal," "We are in a face-off situation," "Dini announces blood and tears," "The President's office prepares to do battle," "The stable door has been closed after the horses have bolted," "Panella shoots point-blank," "Time is of the essence and there is no room for bellyachers," "The government has a long way to go," "We would have lost our battle," and "We are in dire straits." In *La Repubblica* of 28 December 1994 we find that "We need to have our cake and eat it too," "Enough is enough," "May God protect me from my friends," "The Fininvest corporation takes the field once more," "The fat is in the fire," "There's just no help for it," "To cling like a leech," "The wind is changing," "Television takes the lion's share and leaves us the crumbs," "Let's get back on the right track," "The ratings have gone through the floor," "To lose the thread of the tale," "Keep an ear to the market," "Came out of it in bad shape," "The thorn in the side," "To render the honors of war"... It's not journalism, it's hackwork. All things considered, one wonders whether these clichés are more or less transparent than our "parallel convergences," the meaning of which the Red Brigades at least understood and acted upon accordingly.

Note that of these commonplaces, good for the "folks," half came from the writers of the articles and half from politicians' quotes. As you can see, to use another platitude, "the net is closing in," and we are focusing on a diabolical alliance in which we do not know who are the corrupt and who the corrupters.

We have reached the end, therefore, of the hoary debate on objectivity and cryptic language. New problems are appearing. What are they and how did they come into being?

The Daily Becomes a Weekly

In the sixties, newspapers were not as yet suffering from the competition of television. But Achille Campanile, during a conference on television held in Grossetto in September 1962, was struck by a brilliant intuition. At one time the papers were the first to give a piece of news, then other publications stepped in and took the story further; the newspaper was a telegram that finished with "Letter follows." By 1962, the telegraphic news item was given at eight in the evening by the television news. The next day's newspaper ran the same news item: it was a letter that ended with "Telegram follows, or rather, precedes."

Why was a comic genius like Campanile the

only one to notice this paradoxical situation? Because at that time Italian television was limited to one or two channels considered to be under the control of the government, and therefore it was not considered (and largely was not) a reliable source. The newspapers had more to say, and it was said less vaguely. Comedians sprang from the cinema or the clubs, and they did not always make it onto television; political communication took place on the hustings, face to face, or through posters on walls. A study of televised political rallies, made in the sixties, established through an analysis of numerous party broadcasts that, in an attempt to tailor his proposals to the average television viewer, the representative of the Communist Party ended up saying things that were very similar to the remarks made by the representative of the Christian Democratic Party—that is, any differences were all but ironed out as each politician tried to appear as neutral and reassuring as possible. Therefore the polemics, the political struggle, took place elsewhere, and mostly in the newspapers.

Then came the quantitative (the number of channels grew more and more) and qualitative leap; even within the bosom of the national television network there were three separate channels, each with a different political orientation. Satire, the heated debate, and the scoop factory became the province of television, which even broke down the sex taboo, so that some programs broadcast at eleven in the evening were far bolder than the monastic covers of magazines like *Espresso* or *Panorama,* which stopped just north of the gluteus maximus. Still in the early sixties, I recall publishing a review of American talk shows, seen as the loci of civilized, witty conversation capable of keeping viewers glued to the screen until late at night, and I made an impassioned appeal that the format be adopted by Italian television. Thereafter, talk shows assumed a more and more triumphal presence on Italian TV screens, but not only did they encourage a decidedly forthright language (and, to tell the truth, a development of this kind occurred at least in part in the talk shows of other countries), they soon became the scene of violent clashes, occasionally even physical ones.

So television became the primary source of the diffusion of news, and this left the dailies with only two options. As for the first of these possible courses (which I define for now only as "broadened attention") I shall have more to say later, but I think it can be said that most of the daily papers took the second way: they took on the features of weeklies. Daily papers have become more and more like weeklies, devoting an enormous amount of space to variety, society, political gossip, and the world of entertainment in general. This has sparked a crisis for the quality weeklies (in Italy these were *Panorama, Epoca, Europeo,* and *Espresso*), which has left them with two alternatives: either to take on the characteristics of monthlies (but by now there are specialist monthlies—on yachting, watches, cookery, computers—with their own loyal and certain market) or to invade the field of gossip that previously belonged, and still does, to the middlebrow weeklies, *Gente* or *Oggi* for fans of royal weddings, or lowbrow products like *Novella 2000, Stop,* and *Eva Express* for devotees of the extramarital affairs of showbiz personalities and hunters of breasts bared in the intimacy of the bathroom.

But quality weeklies can descend to the low or middle bracket too, which they do in their closing pages—it is toward the end of the magazine that you find the boobs, the affectionate friendships, and the nuptials. However, by doing this they lose the physiognomy of their own readership; the closer a quality weekly gets to the middle or low bracket, the more it acquires a readership that is not its traditional one. It no longer knows whom it is addressing, and a crisis sets in; circulation goes up, but the magazine loses its identity. On the other hand, weeklies have been dealt a lethal blow by the weekly supplements issued by the dailies. There is only one solution for weeklies—to follow in the footsteps of those quality publications, like the *New Yorker,* which offer lists of shows, sophisticated cartoons, brief anthologies of poetry, and even lengthy pieces of up to fifty pages on the life of a doyen of American publishing like Helen Wolff. An alternative would be to follow *Time* or *Newsweek,* which accept being weeklies that talk about events already dealt with by the dailies and the television, but cover these events with concise summaries or in-depth dossiers written by teams of journalists, each of which requires months of planning and work, not to mention documentation so excruciatingly meticulous that these weeklies seldom have to publish letters of rebuttal regarding matters of fact. But even an article for the *New Yorker* is commissioned months beforehand, and then if it is judged unsuitable, the author is paid just the same (and paid very well) and the article is thrown away. This type of weekly has extremely high costs and can exist only for a global English-speaking market, not for a limited Italian-speaking market in which readership figures are still discouraging.

Consequently weeklies are obliged to pursue dailies, along the same road, and each one tries to outdo the other to win over the same readers. This explains why the glorious *Europeo* is closing, *Epoca* is trying desperately to find an alternative route by maintaining itself with television launches, while *Espresso* and *Panorama* are struggling to differentiate themselves. They are different, but the public is less and less aware of this. I frequently meet acquaintances, cultivated ones too, who compliment me on the fine weekly column I write for *Panorama,* and, they assure me with adulation, they buy *Panorama* and only *Panorama* in order to read my column—which, by the way, appears in *Espresso* and not in *Panorama.*

The Ideology of Entertainment

And the dailies? To look like weeklies they increase the number of pages, to increase them they battle for more advertisers, to accommodate more ads they make further increases in the number of pages and invent the supplements; to fill all those pages they have to find something to talk about, and to do that they must go beyond straight news items (which, moreover, have already been ceded to television), and so they take on more and more features typical of weeklies, transforming what is not news into news.

One example. Some months ago, on receiving a prize at Grinzane, I was introduced by my colleague and friend Gianni Vattimo. Those who have an interest in philosophy know that my standpoint is different from Vattimo's, and that nonetheless we respect each other. Others know that we have been close friends since our youth, and enjoy ribbing each other on every convivial occasion. That day Vattimo had opted to go the convivial route. He made an affectionate and witty introduction, and I responded in an equally playful fashion, emphasizing with witticisms and paradoxes our perennial differences of opinion. The following day an Italian newspaper devoted an entire page in its arts section to the clash at Grinzane that supposedly marked, according to the columnist, the birth of a new and dramatic rift in Italian philosophy. The author of the article knew perfectly well that this was not news, not even arts news. He had simply *created a story* that did not exist. I leave it to the reader to find equivalent examples in the political field. But the arts example is an interesting one: the newspaper had to construct a story because it had to fill too many pages devoted to the arts, variety, and society, pages dominated by the ideology of entertainment.

Now let's take a look at the *Corriere* (44 pages) and *La Repubblica* (54 pages) of Monday, 23 January 1995. As the pages of the *Corriere* are more closely written, the quantity of material is the same. Monday is a difficult day because there is no fresh political or economic news, and that leaves sports news at most. That day, we were in the middle of a government crisis in Italy, so our dailies could dedicate their lead articles to the duel between Lamberto Dini and Silvio Berlusconi. A massacre in Israel on "Auschwitz Day" made it possible to fill most of the front page, with the addition of the Andreotti affair and, for the *Corriere,* the death of Rose Kennedy. There was also some news from Chechnya. How to fill up the remaining pages? The two newspapers devoted, respectively, 7 and 4 pages to local news, 14 and 7 pages to sports, 2 and 3 pages to the arts, 2 and 5 pages to the economy, and from 8 to 9 pages to items on society, entertainment, and television. In both papers, out of 32 pages at least 15 were devoted to articles typical of weeklies.

Now let's take the *New York Times* of the same Monday. Out of 53 pages, 16 dealt with sports, 10 with metropolitan problems, and 10 with the economy. That left 17 pages. There was no crisis in progress in the States, and Washington did not require much space, so that the 5 pages of the "National Report" dealt with internal affairs. Then, after the massacre in Israel, I found at least ten articles on Peru, Haiti, Cuban refugees, Rwanda, Bosnia, Algeria, an international conference on poverty, Japan in the aftermath of the earthquake, and the case of Bishop Gaillot. There followed two pages of closely written commentary and political analyses.

The two Italian papers did not mention Peru, Haiti, Cuba, or Rwanda. And even if we admit that the first three interest Americans more than Europeans, in any case it is clear that there were stories concerning international current affairs that the Italian papers dropped in order to increase the sections devoted to entertainment and television. The *New York Times* devoted two pages to media business because it was Monday, but this was composed of reflections and economic analyses of the industry rather than of gossip about show business personalities.

Dailies and TV

By now the Italian press is a slave to television. It is TV that sets, as they say, the agenda of the press. There is no press in the world where television news ends up on the front page, unless Clinton or Mitterrand made a televised address the previous evening, or the CEO of a national network was fired.

And don't tell me that the pages have to be filled somehow. Take the *New York Times* of Sunday, 22 January. All in all there were 569 pages, including ads, the Book Review, the weekly variety section, travel, automobiles, etc. Let's take a look at the part where they talk about television—which is undoubtedly a domestic appliance that occupies a lot of space in the American collective imagination. Television is dealt with on page 32 of the arts and entertainment supplement, where there is a thoughtful piece on racial stereotypes in the programs, and a long review of a fine documentary on volcanoes. Then, obviously, there is the program guide, but the topic of television does not reappear even in the people-and-variety supplement. So it's not true that it is necessary to talk about television in order to fill pages and interest the public. It is a choice, not a necessity. On that same day the Italian press devoted a good deal of space to a program hosted by TV comic Piero Chiambretti (which had not yet been broadcast, and was therefore getting free publicity), in which the central news was that Chiambretti and his camera team had tried to get into the university lecture hall where I was holding a lesson, and I—out of respect for the place and its function—denied him permission to do so. If this was news (because it really would be news if some sanctuary were to remain televisually virgin), it was news worth no more than a couple of lines.

And what if some politician, TV cameras at the ready, had knocked on the door of that lecture hall, and I had requested him to desist? Without entering the hall, and without appearing on television, he would have ended up on the front pages of the papers. In Italy, politicians set the agenda of journalistic priorities by stating something on television (even by letting it be known that such a statement is to be made), and on the following day the press does not talk of events that actually occurred in the country, but rather of what was said about them or could have been said about them on television. Would that that were all, because there is no doubt that a provocative remark made by a politician on TV has by now taken the place of a formal press conference. The fact is, among political news items, Italian newspapers also give front-page space to a bout of face slapping between a gossip columnist and an art critic.

Italy is certainly the country in which, more than any other, the life of television is closely bound up with political life, otherwise there would be no debate about *par condicio,* and this was the case even in the days of Bernabei,[2] before Fininvest[3] appeared on the horizon. The press, therefore, has to account for this bond. A foreign friend drew my attention to the fact that, on Sunday, 29 January 1995, *La Repubblica* (front page and page 7) and the *Corriere* (page 5) both ran a story over several columns on Piero Chiambretti's historic announcement: "I'm not quitting" (and this only because TV journalist Michele Santoro had made a provocative statement about the matter the previous day). Certainly, the career decisions of a comic should not be front-page news, especially if the comic in question has decided *not* to quit his program. If news is man bites dog and not dog bites man, then this was a case of dog that apparently had not bitten anyone. However, we all know that behind that debate, which also involved Enzo Biagi,[4] there lurked a feeling of unease, a polemic with a markedly political flavor. We ought to say that the press was obliged to put it on the front page, out of no fault of its own but as a

---

[2]A former chairman of RAI TV, Italy's national network, whose position was decidedly conservative.

[3]The powerful information and entertainment conglomerate owned by Silvio Berlusconi, TV magnate, former prime minister, and now the leader of Italy's centrist Forza Italia party.

[4]One of the grand old men of Italian journalism.

result of the Italian situation. Yet I would suggest that the Italian situation is what it is partly because of the press.

Well before these events, the press, in order to attract the television public, had set up television as the preferred political space, thus publicizing its own natural competitor beyond all measure. Politicians put two and two together: they chose television and adopted its ways and its language, certain that only by so doing would they attract the attention of the press.

The press has politicized entertainment to an undue extent. So it was an obvious move for a politician to try to get himself noticed by taking the porn star Cicciolina into parliament; and the case of Cicciolina is a typical one because, out of instinctive prudery, television had not given the porn star the space that the press immediately gave her.

The Interview

While it depends on TV for its agenda, the press has also decided to emulate TV style. The most typical way of giving any kind of news—political, literary, scientific—has become the interview. The interview is obligatory in TV, where you cannot talk about people without showing them, but it is an instrument that the press once used with great parsimony. Interviewing people means giving your space to them in order to let them say what *they* want. All we need do is think of what happens when an author publishes a book. Readers expect the press to provide a judgment and an orientation, and they trust the opinion of a well-known critic or the good name of the publication. But today a newspaper is considered a failure if it fails to run an interview with the author in question. What is an interview with the author? Inevitably, self-promotion. It is exceedingly rare for an author to say that he or she has written a disgraceful book. The norm is an implicit form of blackmail (and I would point out that this happens in other countries too): "If you don't grant the interview, we won't even run a review." But then the newspaper, content with the interview, frequently forgets the review. In any case the reader has been defrauded; publicity has taken precedence over or even replaced critical judgment, and often critics, when they finally write something, no longer discuss the book, but rather what the author had to say about it in the course of various interviews.

There is all the more reason for an interview with a politician to be an act of a certain importance: either it is sought by the politician, who wants to use the newspaper as a vehicle—and it is up to the newspaper to decide whether to grant this space or not—or it is sought by the newspaper, which wants to delve further into a certain position adopted by the politician. A significant interview has to take a lot of time, and the interviewee (as happens in virtually all the world) then has to see the quotes, in order to avoid misunderstandings or rebuttals. Today, the newspapers serve up about a dozen interviews a day in which interviewees say what they have already said to other newspapers; but in order to beat the competition, the interview for newspaper A has to be spicier than the one given to newspaper B. The game, therefore, is to wring from the politician a half admission that, artfully emphasized, will trigger a scandal.

So is the politician, on the scene again the following day to retract his statements of the day before, a victim of the press? Then we ought to say to him: "Why do you play along, instead of adopting the efficacious technique of *no comment*?" A few months ago it appeared that Umberto Bossi had chosen this path when he forbade his group in parliament to talk to journalists. A losing strategy, because it exposed him to attacks from the press? A winning strategy, because it won him at least two days of full-page articles in all the papers? Parliamentary journalists say that in most cases of statements followed by virulent rebuttals, it is the politician who has really made that half statement, precisely because the newspapers would publish it, providing them with an opportunity to deny it the following day, having in the meantime launched a *ballon d'essai,* and having successfully hit home with an insinuation or a threat. Upon which one feels like asking the parliamentary journalist, victim of the astute politician: "Why do you play along, why don't you demand that politicians check and endorse the quotes?"

The answer is simple. In this game each party has something to gain and nothing to lose. It is a game played at a dizzying pace, with statements following one another day after day. The result is that the reader loses count and forgets what has been said. By way of compensation the newspaper runs the story with a screaming headline, and the politician cashes in on the situation according to plan. It is a *pactum sceleris* at the expense of the reader and the citizen. But like all crime, in the end it doesn't pay: the price, both for the press and the politician, is unreliability and a "who cares?" reaction from the man on the street.

Interviews have been made more appetizing by the arrival, as we mentioned before, of a radical change in political language, which, by adopting the style of TV debates and TV donnybrooks, is no longer circumspect, but rather picturesque and immediate. For a long time we complained about Italian politicians and their habit of reading out frugal and obscure statements from a slip of paper, and how we admired those American politicians who seemed to speak off the cuff into the microphones, even managing to slip in a few witty quips. Well, in reality things were quite different. Most of them had taken courses in the various "speech centers" of American universities; they followed and still follow the rules of a public-speaking technique that is apparently improvised, but actually regulated with inch-perfect precision. Apart from gaffes, their remarks were and still are taken from special handbooks, or prepared at night by teams of ghostwriters.

Having shrugged off the ornate style of public speaking in the First Republic, the politicians of Italy's Second Republic really do improvise. They talk in a way that is often more comprehensible but frequently unrestrained. Needless to say, for the newspapers, especially if they need to adopt the style of a weekly, all this is manna from heaven. If I may be forgiven an irreverent comparison, this is a typical barroom psychological ploy: someone has one too many and says something incautious, and the entire company does its best to egg him on until he goes clear over the top. This is the dynamic of provocation typical of talk shows, and it also applies to relations between politicians and journalists. Half the phenomena that we now define as the "embitterment of the political struggle" spring from this uncontrollable dynamic. Of course, as I said before, in the dizzying succession of news items, readers forget the specific statement. What lingers on to affect social mores is the tone of the debate, the conviction that anything goes.

The Press Talks about the Press

In this feverish hunt for statements, newspapers deal more and more often with what other newspapers are saying. It is more and more common to find an article in newspaper A announcing an interview due to appear the following day in newspaper B. It is more and more common to find letters of rebuttal sent in by people who say they have never given a statement to newspaper A, which is followed by replies from journalists who state they read the reply in an interview given to newspaper B, without bothering to consider the fact that B might have taken the item indirectly from newspaper C.

When it is not talking about television, the Italian press talks about itself; it has learned from television, which in the main talks about television. Instead of arousing worried indignation, this anomalous situation suits politicians, who find it useful when every statement they make to a single medium is amplified by the sounding board composed of all the media put together. In this way the mass media are transformed from a window on the world into a mirror, and viewers and readers survey a political world lost in contemplation of itself, like the queen in "Snow White."

Who Makes Scoops Today?

Espresso has often launched epoch-making campaigns, the first of which is still renowned: "Corrupt capital, corrupt nation." But what was the technique behind these campaigns? At home I have only one complete year of issues of *Espresso,* 1965, and I leafed through them the other day. From issue number 1 to number 7 the articles ranged from politics to society, and there were no extraordinary revelations. But in number 7 there was a report by Jannuzzi, "Saint Peter's Withholding Tax," in which the Vatican was accused of having evaded, over a three-year period, tax payments amounting to 40 billion lire—with the agreement of the Italian government. At that time the Second Vatican Council was in progress, article 7 of the constitution was once more in question, and the topic was red-hot. Number 8 of the magazine ran nothing on the tax story. Instead there was an article on Hochhuth's *The Deputy,* the performance of which had been vetoed by police authorities in Rome, accompanied by an article by Eugenio Scalfari. There was also an unsigned piece containing inside information about the Vatican Council. Without the reader's becoming aware of it the first time around, the magazine went back to the topic of the *Deputy* in Sandro De Feo's theater column. Number 9 began with a long behind-the-scenes piece by Camilla Cederna on the Vatican Council, which was continued in number 13.

Only in number 13, two months later, did there appear an article by Livio Zanetti, in which he broached the political problem of the revision of the Concordat, and only at the end was the problem linked to that of the alleged Vatican tax scam. This topic returned in number 14, but without big front-page headlines. In number 15 the Church was featured with an article by Falconi on rebel priests and another on varieties of Catholic nonconformism. A front-page editorial assessing the political importance of socialist leader Pietro Nenni's visit to the Vatican did not appear until number 16. Would the Italian state be capable of making its rights respected? Number 18 witnessed the beginning of a new probe, on the mysteries of the law.

The magazine clearly had a strategy; it knew it could not cry wolf every week, so it used measured tones, doling the news out sparingly, allowing readers to form their own opinions gradually, letting the political classes feel the weight of discreet but constant monitoring, and making it clear that, if need be, it could take the lid off things once more.

Could a modern weekly behave the same way? No:

1. In terms of its circulation and layout, the *Espresso* of those days catered to the ruling classes; today it has at least five times as many readers. It can no longer employ the technique of subtle, progressive, and gradual insinuation.

2. Today, the initial scoop would be picked up and amplified by the rest of the press and the other media, and in order to continue running the story, the weekly would have to raise its sights right away, and find more and more explosive

news, even if this meant pumping up data that had not been adequately checked out.

3. In the world of politics, and when featured on TV, treatment of the topic would soon be on a par with a brawl. The subject of the news would no longer be the suspicion of tax fraud, or a problem with the Concordat, but the picturesque clash that would have been triggered by these problems—and the weekly would talk only of how other newspapers or television news programs were approaching the issue.

4. Finally, among the elements responsible for the transformation of the press, we cannot avoid considering the new attitude shown by the judiciary. The press used to intervene in places political forces kept silent about, and into which the judiciary could not see. After the "Clean Hands" scandal the judiciary was handing out so many indictments on all levels that the press was left with very little to reveal. All it could do was report (or anticipate, in a frenetic hunt for "leaks") the indictments that emerged from the courts, or turn the rules on their head and expose the judiciary, but even here all it could do was follow television's lead.

Whereas newspapers once had to send their spies into the corridors of power in Rome to wrangle cautious admissions out of people in the know, today if anything they have to guard against people who procure unsolicited, fat dossiers for them, whose contents, if not thoroughly checked out, are unwittingly amplified by the newspapers, which emerge as dupes and suffer a consequent loss of credibility. Newspapers now have to play a defensive game, parrying blows from outside.

Not that things go much differently elsewhere. In France, for example, there have recently been complaints that the struggle to get a scoop at all costs has violated the jealously guarded privacy of the president of the republic. The consequences of this race for scoops is revealed by a comparison between Nixon and Clinton.

Before the *Washington Post*'s Watergate probe there had never been any attacks, other than political ones, on the presidency and its honorability. If we consider the extent of the deception itself, Nixon could easily have got around the problem by accusing overzealous associates. But he made the mistake of leading off with a lie. At that point the press campaign staked everything on the fact that the president of the United States had lied, and Nixon fell in the end not because he was indirectly guilty of a break-in, but because he was guilty of mendacity. The press's decision was therefore specific, accurate, and calibrated, and that was precisely why it was successful. What made the anti-Clinton campaign far more weak and disjointed is that these days we must have a scoop a day, and in order to have this no one hesitates to attribute to Bill and Hillary malfeasance of all kinds—from property speculation to using state funds to buy cat food. Overkill. Public opinion is disturbed by this, and remains basically skeptical. The final result, in the United States too, is an embitterment of the political struggle; a leader is replaced only if his opponents manage to have him jailed.

What to Do?

If it is to avoid these contradictions, the press is left with two solutions, both difficult, because even foreign newspapers that until now have opted for one or the other have had to change in some way, to adapt to changing times.

The first is the "Fijian way." In 1990 I found myself in the Fiji islands for almost a month, and last year I was in the Caribbean for about the same length of time. On the little islands where I stayed, all I could read was the local daily newspaper: eight or twelve pages, most of which was made up of ads for restaurants and items of local news. Yet I was in Fiji when the Gulf War broke out, and while I was in the Caribbean the first storm clouds were gathering over the Berlusconi administration in Italy. Well, I managed to stay abreast of all the essential facts. These extremely modest papers, working only with agency messages, managed to give in a few lines all the most important news of the previous day. At that distance I understood that what that newspaper did not talk about was not so important after all.

For a newspaper, following the Fijian way naturally means a dramatic fall in sales. The paper would become a bulletin for an elite like those people who read the stock-exchange news, because understanding the importance of a news item given in an essential fashion requires an educated eye. However, this would also be a calamity for political life, which would lose the critical function of the press. Superficial politicians might think that at this point television would suffice for their needs. But television, like every form of entertainment, burns things out. Political figures like Bella Abzug last longer than popular singers like Frankie Laine. A political class also grows and matures through the kind of wide-ranging, calm, and thoughtful dialogue that only relations with the press can permit. And the political class has everything to lose (with only a few short-term advantages—take the money and run) from a daily press turned weekly and modeled wholly on TV.

The other way would be what I call "broadened attention"—where the daily newspaper gives up trying to become a weekly variety magazine in favor of becoming an austere and reliable mine of news about everything that is happening in the world. It will not only cover the coup d'état that occurred the day before in some Third World country but also will have devoted continuous attention to events in that country, even those events that are still incubating. It will explain to readers why (for which economic, political, or even national interests) it is necessary to keep a watch on what is happening down there. But this kind of daily press requires a slow education of the reader; today, in Italy, a daily of this type would lose its readers before it managed to educate them. Even the *New York Times,* which has an educated readership and a singular position in New York, is now losing readers to the lighter and highly colorful *USA Today.*

But other things could happen. With developments in telematics and interactive TV, soon each one of us could set up and print at home, using a TV remote control, his own essential daily newspaper, choosing from a myriad of fonts. The dailies might die—but not the publishers of dailies, who would sell information at slashed prices. But a homemade paper could say only what users are interested in, and would cut them off from a flow of potentially stimulating information, judgments, and alerts; it would rob them of the chance to pick up, on leafing through the rest of a conventional newspaper, unexpected or undesired news. We would have an elite of extremely well-informed users, who know where and when to look for news, and a mass of information subproletarians, content with knowing that a calf with two heads has been born in their district, and ignoring the rest of the world. Which is what already happens with the American newspapers that are not published in New York, San Francisco, Los Angeles, Washington, and Boston.

This too would be a calamity for politicians, obliged to fall back on television alone. We would have a regime like that of a plebiscitary republic, where the electors would react only in the emotion of the moment, program by program, hour by hour. This might strike some as an ideal situation: then, however, not the individual politician but the groups themselves, the movements, would enjoy careers as brief as those of fashion models.

True, this leaves the Internet of the future, and politicians like Al Gore have understood this for some time. Information is diffused through countless independent channels, the system is headless and uncontrollable, everyone discusses with everyone else, and does not merely react emotionally to the survey in real time, but chews over exhaustive messages discovered bit by bit, builds relationships, and enters into discussions over and above parliamentary dialectics or hoary journalistic polemics.

But, and at least for many years:

1. Telematic networks will remain instruments for a cultured and youthful elite—not for Catholic housewives, not for the victims of social discrimination catered to by the refounded Communist Party, not for the pensioners whose cause is championed by the Democratic Party

of the Left, and not for the middle-class woman who demonstrates in support of the Freedom Alliance. In making this threat I am joking, but there is an element of truth here. For the time being, the telematic network gives power not to you politicians and your traditional electors, but rather to my students, who will establish privileged links with the yuppies of Wall Street.

2. There is no guarantee that these networks will remain headless, free of all control from above. We are already nearing gridlock, and tomorrow some Big Brother could gain control of the access channels, and then what price the debate on the *par condicio*?...

3. The immensity of the information these networks permit could lead to censorship by excess. The Sunday edition of the *New York Times* really does contain "all the news that's fit to print," yet it's not that different from the *Pravda* of Stalin's day, because—given that it is not possible to read the whole thing in seven days—it is as if the news it gives were censored. The excess of information leads either to casual criteria of decimation or to discriminating choices granted, once more, to a highly educated elite.

How to conclude? I believe that the press, in the traditional sense of dailies and weeklies made of paper, which one willingly buys at the newsstand, still has a fundamental function—not only for the civil progress of a country but also for our satisfaction and the pleasure of being accustomed, for some centuries now, to consider reading the daily papers, as Hegel suggested, the equivalent of morning prayers for modern man.

But the way things are going today, the Italian press betrays in its own columns a disquiet it is aware of but cannot banish. Since, as we have seen, the alternatives are difficult, what is required is a slow transformation, one that the world of politics cannot afford to remain extraneous to. For reasons we have seen, the daily press cannot be expected to eliminate altogether the process by which it adopts the features of weeklies. But we should not encourage it to report only gossip gathered in the centers of power, or rash off-the-cuff outpourings. For the risk of a collapse is common to all.

Just for a start, it often happens that a politician sends the newspapers an article that appears with the legend "So-and-so is writing in a personal capacity." Right, this is an aid to reflection, and an acceptance of responsibility for one's own statements. Let us ask politicians to read over every interview and endorse the quotes. They will appear less frequently in the papers, but when they do, they will be taken seriously. Newspapers too will benefit from this, because they will no longer be condemned to reporting only emotional outbursts drawn out over one drink and the next. And how will the Italian press fill these gaps? Perhaps by searching for other news, in the rest of the world that does not lie between the Chamber of Deputies and the Senate—places that billions of people could not care less about. Yet we must care about these billions of people. The press must say more about them, and not only because many of our fellow citizens are working with them directly. It is, after all, on their development and their crises that the future of our own society depends.

This is an invitation, addressed to both the press and the world of politics, to look more at the world and less in the mirror.

Ur-Fascism

In 1942, when I was ten, I won the first prize at the *Ludi Juveniles,* a compulsory open competition for all young Italian Fascists—that is to say, for all young Italians. I had written a virtuoso piece of rhetoric in response to the essay title "Should We Die for the Glory of Mussolini and the Immortal Destiny of Italy?" My answer was in the affirmative. I was a smart kid.

Then in 1943 I discovered the meaning of the word "freedom." I shall tell that story at the end of this speech. At the time "freedom" did not yet mean "liberation."

I spent two of my earliest years surrounded by SS, Fascists, and Resistance fighters all busily shooting at one another, and I learned how to dodge bullets. It wasn't bad training.

In April 1945 the partisans took Milan. Two days later they arrived in the little town where I lived. It was a joyous moment. The main square was crowded with people singing and waving flags, calling loudly for Mimo, the leader of the local Resistance movement. A former sergeant in the

Carabinieri, Mimo had thrown his lot in with the followers of Badoglio and had lost a leg in one of the first clashes. He appeared on the balcony of the town hall, pale; with one hand, he tried to calm the crowd. I was waiting for him to begin his speech, given that my entire early childhood had been marked by Mussolini's great historic speeches, the most important parts of which we used to memorize at school. Silence. Mimo's voice was hoarse, you could hardly hear him. He said: "Citizens, friends. After so many painful sacrifices... here we are. Glory to those who fell for freedom." That was it. He went back inside. The crowd gave a shout, the partisans raised their weapons and fired into the air in festive mood. We kids rushed to collect the shell cases, precious collector's items, but I had also learned that freedom of speech means freedom from rhetoric.

Some days later I saw the first American soldiers. They were African-Americans. The first Yankee I met was a black man, Joseph, who introduced me to the wonders of Dick Tracy and L'il Abner. His comics were in color and smelled good.

One of the officers (a Major or Captain Muddy) was billeted in a villa owned by the family of two of my classmates. It was a home away from home for me in that garden where some ladies were clustered around Captain Muddy, talking in sketchy French. Captain Muddy was a well-educated man and knew a little French. So my first image of the American liberators, after all those pale faces in black shirts, was that of a cultivated black man in a yellow green uniform saying: "*Oui, merci beaucoup, Madame, moi aussi j'aime le champagne*..." Unfortunately there was no champagne, but Captain Muddy gave me my first chewing gum and I chewed it all day long. At night I would put the gum in a glass of water, to keep it fresh for the next day.

In May we heard that the war was over. Peace gave me a curious feeling. I had been told that permanent war was the normal condition for a young Italian. Over the following months I discovered that the Resistance was not a local phenomenon but a European one. I learned exciting new words like "*reseau*," "*maquis*," "*armée secrète*," "*Rote Kapelle*," and "*Warsaw ghetto*." I saw the first photographs of the Holocaust, and I learned what this meant even before I learned the word. I realized what it was we had been liberated from.

Some people in Italy today wonder if the Resistance had any real military impact on the course of the war. For my generation the question is irrelevant: we immediately understood the moral and psychological significance of the Resistance. It was a source of pride to know that we Europeans had not waited for liberation passively. I think that for the young Americans who were paying their tribute of blood for our freedom it was not useless to know that behind the lines there were Europeans who were already paying their debt.

Some Italians now say that the legend of the Resistance is a Communist lie. True, the Communists did exploit the Resistance as if it were their own private property, given that they played a primary role in it; but I recall partisans who wore kerchiefs of different colors.

Glued to the radio, I would pass the nights—with the windows closed, the blackout made the tiny space around the radio the only halo of light—listening to the messages that Radio London broadcast to the partisans. They were at once cryptic and poetic ("The sun also rises," "The roses will bloom"), and most of them were "messages for Franchi." Someone whispered to me once that Franchi was the leader of one of the most powerful clandestine groups in North Italy, a man of legendary courage. Franchi became my hero. Franchi (whose real name was Edgardo Sogno) was a monarchist, such a fervent anti-Communist that after the war he joined an extreme right-wing group and was accused of having collaborated in a reactionary coup. But what does it matter? Sogno is still the dream of my childhood.[1] The Liberation was a common undertaking achieved by people of different colors.

Today in Italy some people say that the war of liberation was a tragic period of division, and that now we need national reconciliation. The memory

---

[1]A play on words: in Italian, *sogno* means "dream."

of those terrible years ought to be repressed. But repression causes neurosis. While reconciliation means compassion and respect for all those who fought the war in good faith, forgiving does not mean forgetting. I can even admit that Eichmann believed sincerely in his mission, but I do not feel like saying: "Okay, go back and do it again." We are here to remember what happened and to declare solemnly that "they" must never do it again.

But who are "they"?

If we think again of the totalitarian governments that dominated Europe before the Second World War, we can easily say that they are unlikely to return in the same form in different historic circumstances. Mussolini's Fascism was based on the idea of a charismatic leader, on corporativism, on the utopia of the "fateful destiny of Rome," on the imperialistic will to conquer new lands, on inflammatory nationalism, on the ideal of an entirely regimented nation of Blackshirts, on the rejection of parliamentary democracy, and on anti-Semitism. I admit that Alleanza Nazionale, which sprang from the Movimento Sociale Italiano, is certainly a right-wing party, but it has little to do with the old Fascism. Similarly, even though I am worried by the various pro-Nazi movements active here and there in Europe, Russia included, I don't think that Nazism, in its original form, is about to reappear as a movement involving an entire nation.

Nonetheless, even though political regimes can

be overturned, and ideologies criticized and delegitimized, behind a regime and its ideology there is always a way of thinking and feeling, a series of cultural habits, a nebula of obscure instincts and unfathomable drives. Is there then another ghost wandering through Europe (not to mention other parts of the world)?

Ionesco once said that only words count and all the rest is idle chatter. Linguistic habits are often important symptoms of unspoken sentiments.

Allow me therefore to ask why not only the Resistance but the entire Second World War has been defined all over the world as a struggle against Fascism. If you reread Hemingway's *For Whom the Bell Tolls,* you will discover that Robert Jordan identifies his enemies with the Fascists even when he is thinking of the Spanish Falangists.

I yield the floor to Franklin Delano Roosevelt: "The victory of the American people and their allies will be a victory against Fascism and the blind alley of despotism that it represents" (23 September 1944).

During the McCarthy period, Americans who had taken part in the Spanish Civil War were called "premature anti-Fascists"—another way of saying that fighting Hitler in the forties was a moral duty for all good Americans, but fighting against Franco too soon, in the thirties, was suspect. Why was an expression like "Fascist pig" used by American radicals even to indicate a policeman who did not approve of what they smoked? Why didn't they say: "Caugolard pig," "Falangist pig," "Ustasha pig," "Quisling pig," "Ante Pavelić pig," or "Nazi pig"?

Mein Kampf is the complete manifesto of a political program. Nazism had a theory of race and Aryanism, a precise notion of *entartete Kunst* ("degenerate art"), a philosophy of the will to power and of the *Übermensch*. Nazism was decidedly anti-Christian and neo-Pagan, just as Stalin's *Diamat* (the official version of Soviet Marxism) was clearly materialistic and atheist. If by totalitarian we mean a regime that subordinates all individual acts to the state and its ideology, then Nazism and Stalinism were totalitarian regimes.

Fascism was certainly a dictatorship, but it was not wholly totalitarian—not so much for its moderation as for the philosophical weakness of its ideology. Contrary to commonly held belief, Italian Fascism did not have a philosophy of its own. The article on Fascism signed by Mussolini for the *Enciclopedia Treccani* was written or fundamentally inspired by Giovanni Gentile, but it reflected a late-Hegelian notion of the "ethical and absolute state" that Mussolini never completely realized. Mussolini had no philosophy: all he had was rhetoric. He started out as a militant atheist, only to sign the Concordat with the Church and to consort with the bishops who blessed the Fascist banners. In his early anticlerical years, according to a plausible story, he once asked God to strike him dead on the spot, to prove His existence. God evidently had other fish to fry at the time. In subsequent years, Mussolini always mentioned God in his speeches and was not above having himself called "the man of Providence."

It can be said that Italian Fascism was the first right-wing dictatorship to dominate a European country, and that all similar movements later found a sort of common archetype in Mussolini's regime. Italian Fascism was the first to create a military liturgy, a folklore, and even a style of dress—which enjoyed greater success abroad than Armani, Benetton, or Versace today. It was not until the thirties that Fascist movements sprang up in England, with Mosley, and in Latvia, Estonia, Lithuania, Poland, Hungary, Romania, Bulgaria, Greece, Yugoslavia, Spain, Portugal, Norway, and even South America, not to mention Germany. It was Italian Fascism that convinced many European liberal leaders that the new regime was implementing interesting social reforms capable of providing a moderately revolutionary alternative to the Communist threat.

However, this historical precedence does not strike me as sufficient to explain why the word "Fascism" has become a synecdoche, a denomination *pars pro toto* for different totalitarian movements. It is pointless to say that Fascism contained in itself all the elements of successive totalitarian movements, so to speak, "in a quintessential state." On the contrary, Fascism contained no quintessence, and not even a single essence. It was a fuzzy form of totalitarianism. It was not a monolithic ideology, but rather a collage of diverse political and philosophical ideas, a tangle of contradictions. Is it possible to conceive of a totalitarian movement that manages to reconcile monarchy and revolution, the royal army and Mussolini's private militia, the privileges granted the Church and a state education system that extolled violence, total control, and a free market? The Fascist Party came into being proclaiming a new revolutionary order, but it was financed by the most conservative landowners, who were expecting a counterrevolution. The republican Fascism of the early days endured for twenty years, proclaiming its loyalty to the royal family, allowing a "Duce" to soldier on arm-in-arm with a "king" to whom he also offered the title of emperor. But when in 1943 the king sacked Mussolini, the party resurfaced two months later, with the help of the Germans, under the flag of a "social" republic, thus recycling its old revolutionary score, enhanced by a quasi-Jacobin streak.

There was only one Nazi architecture, and one Nazi art. If the architect of the Nazis was Albert Speer, there was no room for Mies van der Rohe. In the same way, under Stalin, if Lamarck was right, there was no room for Darwin. In contrast, there certainly were Fascist architects, but alongside their pseudo Coliseums there also rose new buildings inspired by the modern rationalism of Gropius.

The Fascists had no Zhdanov. In Italy there were two important art prizes: the Premio Cremona was controlled by an uncultivated and fanatical Fascist like Farinacci, who encouraged propagandistic art (I can remember pictures with titles like *Listening to the Duce's Speech on the Radio* and *Mental States Created by Fascism*); and the Premio Bergamo, sponsored by a cultivated and reasonably tolerant Fascist like Bottai, who protected art for art's sake, and the new avant-garde art that had been banned in Germany as corrupt and crypto-Communist, contrary to Nibelungian kitsch, the only art allowed.

The Italian national poet was D'Annunzio, a fop who in Germany or Russia would have found himself in front of a firing squad. He was elevated to the rank of bard to the regime for his nationalism and cult of heroism—with the addition of a strong dash of French decadence.

Let's take futurism. It ought to have been considered an example of *entartete Kunst*, like expressionism, cubism, and surrealism. But the first Italian futurists were nationalists. For aesthetic reasons they backed Italy's entry into the First World War; they celebrated speed, violence, and risk, and in a certain way these aspects seemed close to the Fascist cult of youth. When Fascism identified itself with Ancient Rome and rediscovered rural traditions, Marinetti—who said an automobile was more beautiful than the

Victory of Samothrace, and even wanted to do away with moonlight—was named a member of the Accademia d'Italia, a body that treated moonlight with great respect.

Many of the future partisans and intellectuals of the Communist Party were educated by the GUF, the Fascist association of university students, which was intended to be the cradle of a new Fascist culture. These clubs became a sort of intellectual melting pot in which new ideas circulated without any real ideological control, not so much because party officials were tolerant, but because few of them possessed the intellectual equipment required to keep a check on the clubs.

In the course of those two decades, the poetry of the so-called hermetic school represented a reaction to the pompous style of the regime. These poets were allowed to elaborate their literary protest from inside the ivory tower. The sentiments of the hermetic poets were exactly the opposite of the Fascist cult of optimism and heroism. The regime tolerated this overt, albeit socially imperceptible dissent, because it did not pay sufficient attention to such obscure jargon.

Which does not mean that Italian Fascism was tolerant. Gramsci remained in prison until his death, Matteotti and the Rosselli brothers were murdered, the free press suppressed, the labor unions dismantled, and political dissidents confined to remote islands. Legislative power became a mere sham, and the executive branch of government (which controlled the judiciary, and the mass media too) enacted new laws directly. This body of new law included the race laws (Italy's formal endorsement of the Holocaust).

The inconsistent image I have described here was not due to tolerance: it was an example of political and ideological chaos. But it was "orderly chaos," organized confusion. Fascism was philosophically unsound, but on an emotional level it was firmly anchored to certain archetypes.

We have now come to the second part of my case. There was only one Nazism, and we cannot describe the ultra-Catholic Falangism of Franco as Nazism, given that Nazism is fundamentally pagan, polytheistic, and anti-Christian, otherwise it is not Nazism. On the other hand, you can play the Fascism game many ways, and the name of the game does not change. According to Wittgenstein, what happens with the notion of "Fascism" is what happens with the notion of "play." A game can be competitive or otherwise, it can involve one or more people, it may require some particular skills or none, there may be money at stake or not. Games are a series of diverse activities that reveal only a few "family resemblances."

Let us suppose that there is a series of political groups. Group 1 is characterized by the aspects *abc*, group 2 by *bcd*, and so on. 2 is similar to 1 insofar as they have two aspects in common. 3 is similar to

1	2	3	4
abc	bcd	cde	def

2 and 4 is similar to 3 for the same reason. Note that 3 is also similar to 1 (they share the aspect *c*). The most curious case is that of 4, obviously similar to 3 and 2 but without any characteristic in common with 1. Nevertheless, because of the uninterrupted series of decreasing similarities between 1 and 4, there remains, by virtue of a sort of illusory transitiveness, a sense of kinship between 4 and 1.

The term "Fascism" fits everything because it is possible to eliminate one or more aspects from a Fascist regime and it will always be recognizably Fascist. Remove the imperialist dimension from Fascism, and you get Franco or Salazar; remove the colonialist dimension, and you get Balkan Fascism. Add to Italian Fascism a dash of radical anti-Capitalism (which never appealed to Mussolini), and you get Ezra Pound. Add the cult of Celtic mythology and the mysticism of the Grail (completely extraneous to official Fascism), and you get one of the most respected gurus of Fascism, Julius Evola.

Despite this confusion, I think it is possible to draw up a list of characteristics typical of what I should like to call "Ur-Fascism," or "eternal Fascism." These characteristics cannot be regimented into a system; many are mutually exclusive and are typical of other forms of despotism or fanaticism.

But all you need is one of them to be present, and a Fascist nebula will begin to coagulate.

1. The first characteristic of Ur-Fascism is the *cult of tradition.* Traditionalism is older than Fascism. It was not only typical of Catholic counterrevolutionary thinking after the French Revolution but was born in the late Hellenic period as a reaction to classical Greek rationalism.

   In the Mediterranean basin, the peoples of different religions (all indulgently welcomed into the Roman pantheon) began dreaming of a revelation received at the dawn of human history. This revelation lay for a long time concealed under a veil of languages by now forgotten. It was guarded by Egyptian hieroglyphics, Celtic runes, and the sacred writings, still unknown, of the Asiatic religions.

   This new culture was to be *syncretic.* "Syncretism" is not merely, as the dictionaries say, the combination of different forms of beliefs or practices. A combination like this *must tolerate contradictions.* All the original messages contain a grain of wisdom, and when they seem to be saying different or incompatible things, it is only because they all allude, allegorically, to some original truth.

   Consequently, *there can be no advancement of learning.* The truth has already been announced once and for all, and all we can do is continue interpreting its obscure message. It suffices to take a look at the syllabus of every Fascist movement, and you will find the principal traditionalist thinkers. Nazi gnosis fed on traditionalist, syncretic, and occult elements. The most important theorist of the new Italian right, Julius Evola, mixed the Grail with the Protocols of the Elders of Zion, and alchemy with the Holy Roman Empire. The very fact that, in order to demonstrate its open-minded stance, a part of the Italian right has recently widened its syllabus by putting together De Maistre, Guenon, and Gramsci is glaring evidence of syncretism.

If you browse through the New Age sections in American bookshops, you will even find Saint Augustine, who, as far as I know, was not a Fascist. But putting together Saint Augustine and Stonehenge, now *that* is a symptom of Ur-Fascism.

2. Traditionalism implies the rejection of modernism. Both the Fascists and the Nazis worshiped technology, while traditionalist thinkers usually reject technology as the negation of traditional spiritual values. Nevertheless, although Nazism was proud of its industrial successes, its praise of modernity was only the superficial aspect of an ideology based on "blood and soil" (*Blut und Boden*). The rejection of the modern

world was disguised as a condemnation of the capitalist way of life, but mainly concerned a rejection of the spirit of 1789 (or of 1776, obviously). The Enlightenment and the Age of Reason were seen as the beginning of modern depravity. In this sense, Ur-Fascism can be defined as irrationalism.

3. Irrationalism also depends on the cult of *action for action's sake.* Action is beautiful in itself, and therefore must be implemented before any form of reflection. Thinking is a form of emasculation. Therefore *culture is suspect* insofar as it is identified with critical attitudes. From the statement attributed to Goebbels ("When I hear talk of culture, I take out my pistol") to the frequent use of expressions like "goddamn intellectuals," "eggheads," "radical snobs," "The universities are a den of Communists," suspicion of intellectual life has always been a symptom of Ur-Fascism. The official Fascist intellectuals were mainly committed to accusing modern culture and the liberal intelligentsia of having abandoned traditional values.

4. No form of syncretism can accept criticism. The critical spirit makes distinctions, and distinguishing is a sign of modernity. In modern culture, the scientific community sees dissent as

a tool with which to promote the advancement of learning. For Ur-Fascism, *dissent is betrayal.*

5. Dissent is moreover a sign of diversity. Ur-Fascism grows and seeks a consensus by exploiting and exacerbating the natural *fear of difference.* The first appeal of a Fascist or prematurely Fascist movement is a call against intruders. Ur-Fascism is therefore racist by definition.

6. Ur-Fascism springs from individual or social frustration, which explains why one of the characteristics typical of historic Fascist movements was *the appeal to the frustrated middle classes,* disquieted by some economic crisis or political humiliation, and frightened by social pressure from below. In our day, in which the old "proletarians" are becoming petits bourgeois (and the lumpen proletariat has excluded itself from the political arena), Fascism will find its audience in this new majority.

7. To those with no social identity at all, Ur-Fascism says that their only privilege is the most common privilege of all, that of being born in the same country. This is the origin of nationalism. Moreover, the only ones who can provide the nation with an identity are the enemy. Thus, at the root of Ur-Fascist psychology lies the

obsession with conspiracies, preferably international ones. The disciples must feel that they are under siege. The easiest way to construct a conspiracy is to appeal to *xenophobia.* But conspiracies must also come from the inside: the Jews are usually the best target, because they offer the advantage of being at once both inside and outside. In America, the latest example of this obsession with conspiracies is Pat Robertson's book *The New World Order.*

8. The disciples must feel humiliated by the enemy's vaunted wealth and power. When I was a little boy, they taught me that the English were the "five-meals people," eating more often than the poor but sober Italians. The Jews are wealthy and help one another through a secret network of mutual assistance. But the disciples must nonetheless feel they can defeat the enemy. Thus, thanks to a continual shifting of the rhetorical register, *the enemy is at once too strong and too weak.* Fascist regimes are doomed to lose their wars, because they are constitutionally incapable of making an objective assessment of the enemy's strength.

9. For Ur-Fascism there is no struggle for life but, rather, a "life for struggle." *Pacifism is therefore collusion with the enemy*; pacifism is bad, be-

cause *life is a permanent war.* This, however, brings with it an Armageddon complex: since the enemy can and must be defeated, there must be a last battle, after which the movement will rule the world. Such a *final solution* implies a subsequent era of peace, a Golden Age that contradicts the principle of permanent war. No Fascist leader has ever managed to resolve this contradiction.

10. Elitism is a typical aspect of all reactionary ideologies, insofar as it is basically aristocratic. In the course of history, all forms of aristocratic and militaristic elitism have implied *scorn for the weak.* Ur-Fascism cannot do without preaching a "popular elitism." Every individual belongs to the best people in the world, party members are the best citizens, and every citizen can (or ought to) become a party member. But you cannot have patricians without plebeians. The leader, who is well aware that his power has not been obtained by delegation but was taken by force, also knows that his power is based on the weakness of the masses, who are so weak as to need and deserve a "dominator." Since the group is organized hierarchically (along military lines), each subordinate leader looks down on his inferiors, and each of his inferiors looks down in turn on his own underlings. All this

looking down reinforces the sense of a mass elite.

11. From this point of view, everyone is trained to become a hero. In every mythology the hero is an exceptional being, but in the Ur-Fascist ideology heroism is the norm. This cult of heroism is closely connected to the *cult of death*: there is nothing accidental about the fact that the motto of the Falangists was "*Viva la muerte!*" Normal people are told that death is unpleasant but has to be faced with dignity; believers are told that it is a painful way to attain a supernatural happiness. But the Ur-Fascist hero aspires to death, hailed as the finest reward for a heroic life. The Ur-Fascist hero is impatient to die. In his impatience, it should be noted, he usually manages to make others die in his place.

12. Since both permanent war and heroism are difficult games to play, the Ur-Fascist transfers his will to power onto sexual questions. This is the origin of *machismo* (which implies contempt for women and an intolerant condemnation of nonconformist sexual habits, from chastity to homosexuality). Since sex is also a difficult game to play, the Ur-Fascist hero plays with weapons, which are his ersatz penis: his war games are due to a permanent state of penis envy.

13. Ur-Fascism is based on "qualitative populism." In a democracy the citizens enjoy individual rights, but as a whole the citizens have a political impact only from a quantitative point of view (the decisions of the majority are followed). For Ur-Fascists individuals have no rights, and the "people" is conceived of as a monolithic entity that expresses the "common will." Since no quantity of human beings can possess a common will, the leader claims to be their interpreter. Having lost their power to delegate, the citizens do not act, they are only called upon, *pars pro toto,* to play their role as the people. The people is thus merely a theatrical pretense. For a good example of qualitative populism, we no longer need Piazza Venezia or the stadium in Nuremberg. In our future there looms *qualitative TV* or *Internet populism,* in which the emotional response of a selected group of citizens can be presented and accepted as the "voice of the people." As a result of its qualitative populism, Ur-Fascism *has to oppose "rotten" parliamentary governments.* One of the first things Mussolini said in the Italian parliament was, "I could have transformed this gray and sordid chamber into a bivouac for my soldiers." As a matter of fact, he immediately found a better billet for his soldiery, but shortly after that he dissolved the parliament. Every time a politician casts doubt on

the legitimacy of a parliament because it no longer represents the "voice of the people," there is a suspicion of Ur-Fascism.

14. Ur-Fascism uses newspeak. "Newspeak" was invented by Orwell in *1984*, as the official language of Ingsoc, the English Socialist movement, but elements of Ur-Fascism are common to different forms of dictatorship. All the Nazi and Fascist scholastic texts were based on poor vocabulary and elementary syntax, the aim being to limit the instruments available to complex and critical reasoning. But we must be prepared to identify other types of newspeak, even when they take the innocent form of a popular talk show.

Now that I have listed the possible characteristics of Ur-Fascism, let me come to a conclusion. On the morning of 27 July 1943 I learned from a radio news broadcast that Fascism had collapsed and Mussolini had been arrested. My mother sent me to buy a newspaper. I went to the nearest newsstand and saw that there were newspapers, but the names were different. Moreover, after a quick glance at the headlines, I realized that every newspaper said something different. I bought one at random and read the message printed on the front page, signed by five or six political parties, like Democrazia Cristiana, Partito Comunista, Partito Socialista, Partito d'Azione, and Partito Liberale. Until that moment I had believed that there was only one party in every country, and that in Italy there was only the National Fascist Party. I was discovering that in my country there could be many different parties at the same time. What's more, since I was a smart kid I realized right away that all those parties could not have emerged overnight. Thus I understood that they had already existed as clandestine organizations.

The message celebrated the end of the dictatorship and the return of freedom: freedom of speech, of the press, of political association. My God, I had never read words like "freedom" or "dictatorship" in all my life. By virtue of these words I was reborn as a free Western man.

We must make sure that the sense of these words is not forgotten again. Ur-Fascism is still around us, sometimes in civilian clothes. It would be so easy for us if someone would look out onto the world's stage and say: "I want to reopen Auschwitz, I want the Blackshirts to march through the streets of Italy once more!" Alas, life is not so simple. Ur-Fascism can still return in the most innocent of guises. Our duty is to unmask it and to point the finger at each of its new forms—every day, in every part of the world. Once more I yield the floor to Roosevelt: "I dare to say that if American democracy ceased to progress as a living force, seeking night and day by peaceful means to improve the condition of our citizens, the power of

Fascism would grow in our country" (4 November 1938). Freedom and liberation are never-ending tasks. Let this be our motto: "Do not forget."

And now I should like to close with a poem by Franco Fortini:

On the parapet of the bridge
The heads of hanged men
In the water of the fountain
The drool of hanged men

On the cobbles of the market
The fingernails of men shot down
On the dry grass of the meadow
The teeth of men shot down

Bite the air bite the stones
Our flesh is the flesh of men no more
Bite the air bite the stones
Our hearts are the hearts of men no more.

But we have read the dead men's eyes
And the world's freedom is the gift we bring
While the coming justice is close
Clenched in the hands of the dead.

Migration, Tolerance, and the Intolerable

Migration in the Third Millennium

The year 2000 is almost upon us. I do not intend to discuss whether the new millennium begins midnight 31 December 1999 or 2000, as mathematics and chronology would encourage us to believe that it does. From a symbolic standpoint, both mathematics and chronology are an opinion, and there is no doubt that 2000 is a magical number, whose glamour is hard to resist after all those nineteenth-century novels that hailed the marvels of the year 2000.

On the other hand we know that, even from a chronological point of view, computers and their dating systems will hit a crisis on 1 January 2000 and not on 1 January 2001. Our feelings may be impalpable and erratic, but computers do not make mistakes even when they do make mistakes: if they are wrong about 1 January 2000, then they are right.

For whom is the year 2000 a magical one? For the Christian world, evidently, given that it marks two thousand years from the presumed birth of

Christ (even though we know that Christ was definitely not born in the year 0 of our era). We cannot say "for the Western world," because the Christian world extends to oriental civilizations too, while the so-called Western world includes Israel, which thinks of our system of recording time as the "common era," but keeps a quite different count of the years.

In the seventeenth century the protestant Isaac de la Peyrière observed that Chinese chronologies were much older than Jewish ones and conjectured that original sin involved only the descendants of Adam, not other races, born far earlier. Naturally he was declared to be a heretic, but, immaterial of whether he was right or wrong from a theological point of view, he was reacting to a fact that no one today doubts anymore: the various dating systems in force in different cultures reflect different theogonies and historiographies, and the Christian system is merely one among many (and I should like to point out that the calculation *ab anno Domini* is not as old as people think, because as recently as the early Middle Ages years were counted not from the birth of Christ but from the presumed creation of the world).

I believe that the year 2000 will be celebrated even in Singapore and in Beijing, owing to the influence of the European model on other models. Everyone will probably celebrate the coming of the year 2000, but for most of the peoples of the world this will be a commercial convention, not a profound conviction. If China had a flourishing civilization before our year 0 (and we know that before that date there were other civilizations in the Mediterranean basin; all that has happened is that we have agreed to record the age of Plato and Aristotle as "before Christ"), what does it mean to celebrate the year 2000? It means the triumph of the model that I shall not call "Christian" (because atheists will celebrate 2000 as well), but of the European model that, after Columbus's "discovery" of America—even though American Indians say that they were the ones who discovered us—also became the American model.

When we celebrate the year 2000, what year will it be for Muslims, Australian aborigines, and the Chinese? Of course we could disregard this. The year 2000 is ours, it is a Eurocentric date, our business. But apart from the fact that the Eurocentric model seems to dominate American civilization too—although the American nation includes Africans, Orientals, and Native Americans who do not identify with this model—do we Europeans still have the right to identify ourselves with the Eurocentric model?

Some years ago, upon the constitution of the Académie Universelle des Cultures in Paris, an organization made up of artists and scientists from all over the world, a statute or charter was drawn up. And one of the introductory declarations of this charter, which was also intended to define the scientific and moral duties of this academy, was that the coming millennium would witness a "great cross-breeding of cultures."

If the course of events is not suddenly inverted (and everything is possible), we must prepare ourselves for the fact that in the next millennium Europe will be like New York or some Latin American countries. In New York we see the negation of the "melting pot" concept: different cultures coexist, from Puerto Ricans to Chinese, from Koreans to Pakistanis. Some groups have merged with one another (like Italians and Irish, Jews and Poles), others have kept themselves separate (living in different districts, speaking different languages and following different traditions), and all come together on the basis of some common laws and a common lingua franca, English, which each group speaks insufficiently well. I ask you to bear in mind that in New York, where the so-called white population is on the way to becoming a minority, 42 percent of the whites are Jews and the other 58 percent are of the most disparate origins, and of their number the Wasps are the minority (there are Polish Catholics, Italians, Hispanic-Americans, Irish, etc.).

In Latin America, depending on the country, different phenomena have occurred: sometimes the Spanish colonizers interbred with the Indians, sometimes (as in Brazil) with the Africans too, and sometimes languages and populations known as "Creole" came into being. It is very difficult, even if we think in racial terms, to say whether a Mexican or a Peruvian is of European or Amerindian origin. And it's even harder to decide about, let's say, a Jamaican.

So, the future of Europe holds a phenomenon of this kind, and no racist or backward-looking reactionary will be able to prevent it.

I believe that a distinction must be drawn between the concept of "immigration" and that of "migration." Immigration occurs when some individuals (even many individuals, but in numbers that are statistically irrelevant with respect to the original stock) move from one country to another (like the Italians and the Irish in America, or the Turks today in Germany). The phenomenon of immigration may be controlled politically, restricted, encouraged, planned, or accepted.

This is not the case with migration. Violent or pacific as it may be, it is like a natural phenomenon: it happens, and no one can control it. Migration occurs when an entire people, little by little, moves from one territory to another (the number remaining in the original territory is of no importance: what counts is the extent to which the migrants change the culture of the territory to which they have migrated). There have been great migrations from East to West, in the course of which the peoples of the Caucasus changed the culture and biological heredity of the natives. Then there were the migrations of the "barbarian" peoples that invaded the Roman Empire and created new kingdoms and new cultures called "Romano-barbarian" or "Romano-Germanic." There was European migration toward the American continent, from the East Coast and gradually across to California, and also from the Caribbean islands and Mexico all the way to Tierra del Fuego. Even though this was in part politically planned, I use the term "migration" because the European whites did not adopt the customs and the culture of the natives, but rather founded a new civilization to which even the natives (those who survived) adapted.

There have been interrupted migrations, like those of the Arab peoples who got as far as the Iberian peninsula. There have been forms of migration that were planned and partial, but no less influential for this, like that of Europeans to the East and South (hence the birth of the so-called postcolonial nations), where the migrants nonetheless changed the culture of the autochthonous peoples. I don't think that anyone has so far described a phenomenology of the different types of migration, but migration is certainly different from immigration. We have only immigration when the immigrants (admitted according to political decisions) accept most of the customs of the country into which they have immigrated, while migration occurs when the migrants (whom no one can stop at the frontiers) radically transform the culture of the territory they have migrated to.

Today, after a nineteenth century full of immigrants, we find ourselves faced with unclear phenomena. In a climate marked by pronounced mobility, it is very difficult to say whether a certain movement of people is immigration or migration. There is certainly an unstoppable flow from the south to the north (as Africans and Middle Easterners head for Europe), the Indians have invaded Africa and the Pacific islands, the Chinese are everywhere, and the Japanese are present with their industrial and economic organizations even though they have not moved physically in any significant numbers.

Is it possible to distinguish immigration from migration when the entire planet is becoming the territory of intersecting movements of people? I think it is possible: as I have said, immigration can be controlled politically, but like natural phenomena, migration cannot be. As long as there is immigration, peoples can hope to keep the immigrants in a ghetto, so that they do not mix with the natives. When migration occurs, there are no more ghettos, and intermarriage is uncontrollable.

What Europe is still trying to tackle as immigration is instead migration. The Third World is knocking at our doors, and it will come in even if we are not in agreement. The problem is no longer to decide (as politicians pretend) whether students at a Paris university can wear the chador or how many mosques should be built in Rome. The problem is that in the next millennium (and since I am not a prophet, I cannot say exactly when) Europe will become a multiracial continent—or a "colored" one, if you prefer. That's how it will be, whether you like it or not.

This meeting (or clash) of cultures could lead to bloodshed, and I believe that to a certain extent it will. Such a result cannot be avoided and will last a long time. However, racists ought to be (in theory) a race on the way to extinction. Was there a patrician class in ancient Rome that could not tolerate the idea of Gauls, or Sarmatians, or Jews like Saint Paul becoming Roman citizens, or of an African ascending the imperial throne, as indeed happened in the end? The patricians have been forgotten, defeated by history. Roman civilization was a hybrid culture. Racists will say that this is why it fell, but its fall took five hundred years—which strikes me as time enough for us too to make plans for the future.

Intolerance

Fundamentalism and integralism are usually considered to be closely linked concepts and as the two most obvious forms of intolerance. If I consult two excellent references like the *Petit Robert* and the *Dictionnaire Historique de la Langue Française,* I find in the definition of "fundamentalism" an immediate reference to integralism. Which prompts me to think that all forms of fundamentalism are forms of integralism and vice versa.

But even if this were so, it would not mean that all intolerant people are fundamentalists or integralists. Even though at present we are faced with different forms of fundamentalism while examples of integralism are visible everywhere, the problem of intolerance is deeper and more dangerous.

In historical terms fundamentalism is a hermeneutic principle, linked to the interpretation of a *holy book*. Modern Western fundamentalism was born in Protestant circles in the nineteenth-century United States, and its characteristic feature is the decision to interpret the Scriptures literally, especially with regard to those notions of cosmology whose truth the science of the day seemed to doubt. Hence the frequently intolerant rejection of all allegorical interpretations, and especially of all forms of education that attempted to undermine faith in the biblical text, as occurred with the triumph of Darwinism.

This form of fundamentalist literalism is ancient, and even in the days of the Fathers of the Church there were debates between partisans of the letter and supporters of a suppler hermeneutics, like that of Saint Augustine. But in the modern world strict fundamentalism could only be Protestant, given that in order to be a fundamentalist you have to assume that the truth is given by a certain interpretation of the Bible. In the Catholic world it is the authority of the Church that guarantees the validity of interpretation, and so the Catholic equivalent of Protestant fundamentalism takes if anything the form of traditionalism. I shall omit any consideration of the nature of Muslim and Jewish fundamentalism, which I leave to the experts.

Is fundamentalism necessarily intolerant? On a hermeneutic level it is, but not necessarily on a political one. It is possible to imagine a fundamentalist sect that assumes its own elect to be the privileged possessors of the correct interpretation of the Scriptures, without however indulging in any form of proselytism and consequently without wishing to oblige others to share those beliefs, or to fight for a society based on them. "Integralism," on the other hand, refers to a religious and political position whereby religious principles must become at once the model of political life and the source of the laws of the state. While fundamentalism and integralism are in principle conservative, there are forms of integralism that claim to be progressive and revolutionary. There are Catholic integralist movements that are not fundamentalist, fighting for a society totally inspired by religious principles but without imposing a literal interpretation of the Scriptures, and maybe prepared to accept a theology like that of Teilhard de Chardin.

The nuances can be even subtler. Think of the phenomenon of political correctness in America. This sprang from the desire to encourage tolerance and the recognition of all differences, religious, racial, and sexual, and yet it is becoming a new form of fundamentalism that is affecting everyday language in a practically ritual fashion, and that works on the letter at the expense of the spirit—and so you can discriminate against blind persons provided that you have the delicacy to call them the "sightless," and above all you can discriminate against those who do not follow the rules of political correctness.

And racism? Nazi racism was certainly totalitarian; it had pretensions to being scientific, but there was nothing fundamentalist about the doctrine of race. An unscientific racism like that of Italy's Northern League does not have the same cultural roots of pseudoscientific racism (in reality it has no cultural roots), yet it is racism.

And intolerance? Can it be reduced to these differences and the kinship between fundamentalism, integralism, and racism? There have been nonracist forms of intolerance (like the persecution of the heretics or the intolerance of dissidents in dictatorships). Intolerance is something far deeper, lying at the roots of all the phenomena I am considering here.

Fundamentalism, integralism, and pseudoscientific racism are theoretical positions that presuppose a *doctrine.* Intolerance comes before any doctrine. In this sense intolerance has biological roots, it manifests itself among animals as territoriality, it is based on emotional reactions that are often superficial—we cannot bear those who are different from us, because their skin is a different color; because they speak a language we do not understand; because they eat frogs, dogs, monkeys, pigs, or garlic; because they tattoo themselves...

Intolerance for what is different or unknown is as natural in children as their instinct to possess all they desire. Children are educated gradually to tolerance, just as they are taught to respect the property of others and, even before that, to control their sphincters. Unfortunately, while everyone learns to control his own body, tolerance is a permanent educational problem with adults, because in everyday life we are forever exposed to the trauma of difference. Academics often deal with the doctrines of difference, but devote insufficient attention to uncontrolled intolerance, because it eludes all definition and critical consideration.

Yet the doctrines of difference do not produce uncontrolled intolerance: on the contrary, they exploit a preexisting and diffuse reservoir of intolerance. Take the witch hunts. This phenomenon was a product not of the Dark Ages but of the modern age. The *Malleus Maleficarum* was written shortly after the discovery of America, it was a contemporary of Florentine humanism; Jean Bodin's *Démonomanie des sorciers* came from the pen of a Renaissance man who wrote after Copernicus. My intention here is not to explain why the modern world produces theoretical justifications for witch hunts; all I want to do is point out that this doctrine became successful because popular fear of witches was already a reality. That fear can be found in classical antiquity (Horace), in the edict of King Rotari, and in the *Summa theologica* of Saint Thomas. It was considered a part of everyday life, just as the penal code provides for muggers. Without this popular belief a doctrine of witchcraft and the systematic persecution of witches could never have gained currency.

Pseudoscientific anti-Semitism arose in the course of the nineteenth century and became totalitarian anthropology and industrialized genocide only in the twentieth. But it could never have arisen had an anti-Jewish polemic not been under way for centuries, since the days of the Fathers of the Church, or if common people had not translated anti-Semitism into practice, a situation that endured for hundreds of years wherever there was a ghetto. The anti-Jacobin theories of Jewish conspiracy circulating at the beginning of the nineteenth century did not create popular anti-Semitism, but rather exploited a hatred for difference that already existed.

The most dangerous form of intolerance is precisely the kind that arises in the absence of any doctrine, fueled by elemental drives. This is why it cannot be criticized or curbed by rational argument. The theoretical foundations of *Mein Kampf* can be confuted by a battery of fairly simple arguments, but if the ideas proposed in it have survived and continue to survive all objections, it is because they are founded on uncontrolled intolerance, which is immune to all criticism. I find the intolerance of the Italian Northern League more dangerous than that of Le Pen's Front National. The historical background of Le Pen's movement is characterized by the perfidy of a certain class of right-wing intellectuals, while Northern League leader Bossi has nothing but uncontrolled drives.

Look at what is happening these days in Italy, where twelve thousand Albanians have entered the country in little over a week. The public and official model was one of welcome. Most of those who want to stop this exodus, which could become more than the country can handle, use economic and demographic arguments. But all theories are rendered superfluous by a creeping intolerance that gains new ground with every day that passes.

Uncontrolled intolerance is based on a categorical short circuit that is then leased out to every future racist doctrine: if some of the Albanians who have come to Italy over the past few years have become thieves or prostitutes (and this is true), then all Albanians are thieves and prostitutes.

This is a frightening short circuit, because it constitutes a constant temptation for all of us: all it takes is for someone to steal our baggage at an airport anywhere in the world, and we go back home saying that the people of that country cannot be trusted.

The most frightening form of intolerance is that of the poor, who are the first victims of difference.

There is no racism among the rich. The rich have produced, if anything, the doctrines of racism. The poor, on the other hand, have produced its practice, which is far more dangerous.

Intellectuals cannot fight uncontrolled intolerance, because when faced with pure unthinking animality, thought finds itself defenseless. But it is too late when war is waged on doctrinal intolerance, for when intolerance is transformed into doctrine the war is already lost, and those who ought to fight it become the first victims.

Yet it is here that the challenge lies. To inculcate tolerance in adults who shoot at one another for ethnic and religious reasons is a waste of time. Too late. Therefore uncontrolled intolerance has to be beaten at the roots, through constant education that starts from earliest infancy, before it is written down in a book, and before it becomes a behavioral "skin" that is too thick and too tough.

The Intolerable

There are irritating questions, as when someone asks you what has happened just after you bit your tongue. "What do you think about that?" people ask you at a time in which everyone (with a very few exceptions) thinks the same thing about the Priebke case. And they are almost disappointed when you reply that, obviously, you are indignant and bewildered, because essentially everyone asks this question of everyone else in the hope of hearing a word, an explanation, that might reduce the indignation or bewilderment.[1]

One is almost embarrassed to talk about this, to obtain thus a general consensus so cheaply, honorable men among other honorable men in an arc that spans the gap between the extreme left and the extreme right. As if the Rome Military Tribunal had finally led almost all Italians to agree. We are all on the side of the just.

And what if the Priebke case had implications over and above the individual episode—all things considered, a fairly squalid one (an unrepentant criminal, a fainthearted tribunal)—and involved us on a deeper level? Would it not suggest that not even we are innocent?

We still assess what happened in terms of the laws in force. Under current law perhaps Priebke could have been given a life sentence, but in terms of jurisprudence it cannot even be said that the tribunal's decision was an unthinkable one. There was a criminal who had confessed to a horrible crime, and, as every court must, the tribunal had to see whether there weren't any mitigating circum-

---

[1]Erich Priebke is a former SS officer recently extradited from Argentina to stand trial in Italy for war crimes: reprisals that took the form of a mass execution of civilians at the Ardeatine Caves in Rome. He was absolved on a technicality: the statute of limitations.

stances. Well, those were hard times, Priebke was not a hero but a wretched coward, and even if he had weighed the enormity of the crime, he would have been afraid to pay the consequences of a refusal. He killed an extra five people, but when men are drunk with blood, as we know, they become beasts. He's guilty, all right, but instead of life let's give him a long stretch; justice is saved, the statute of limitations comes into play, and we can close a painful chapter. Would we not have done the same for Raskolnikov, who murdered an old lady, and without any military excuse at that?

We are the ones who have conferred upon the judges a mandate to behave in accordance with the laws in force, and now we present them with an objection, a moral requirement, a passion; and they reply that they are judges, not killers.

Most of the objections turn on the interpretation of preexisting laws. Priebke had to obey orders, because such is the law of a country at war; but no, even the Nazis had laws that allowed them to avoid obeying an unjust order, and then again Priebke should not have been tried under military law, because the SS were a volunteer police corps. But international conventions justify the right to make reprisals; indeed, one may reply, but only in cases of declared war, and there is no evidence that Germany declared war on the Kingdom of Italy, and therefore the Germans, the illegal occupiers of a country with which they were not officially at war, could not complain if someone disguised as a street sweeper blew up one of their convoys.

We shall not get out of this circle until it is decided that when exceptional events occur, humanity cannot afford to apply the laws currently in force, but must shoulder the responsibility of sanctioning new ones.

We still have not drawn all our conclusions regarding the epoch-making event that was the Nuremberg trials. In terms of strict legality or international custom it was an arbitrary act. We had been accustomed to the notion that war was a game with rules, and that at the end of the day the king would embrace his cousin the winner, and then what do they do, take the vanquished and hang them? Sure, reply those who decided upon Nuremberg: we think that in this war some things happened that exceeded the limits of tolerability, and that's why we're changing the rules. But this level of tolerability reflects your values as winners; we had other values, don't you have any respect for them? No, since we won, and since among your values there is the glorification of power, we shall use power: we're going to hang you. But what will happen in future wars? Those who foment them will know that if they lose they will be hanged; let them think about that before they start. But your side committed atrocities too! Yes, but that is what you losers are saying; we are the winners, so *we* are going to hang *you*. And will you take responsibility for this? Yes, we will.

I am against the death penalty, and even if I had captured Hitler, I would have sent him to Alcatraz. So from now on I shall use "hanging" in a symbolic sense, to suggest a hard and solemn punishment. But apart from hanging, the reasoning behind Nuremberg is flawless. Faced with intolerable conduct, we must have the courage to change the rules, laws included. Can a tribunal in Holland judge the conduct of someone in Serbia or Bosnia? According to the old rules, it can't; according to the new ones, it can.

At the end of 1982 there was a conference in Paris on intervention, which was attended by jurists, military personnel, pacifist volunteers, philosophers, and politicians. By what right and according to what criteria of prudence can we intervene in the affairs of another state when it is held that something is happening there that is intolerable in the view of the international community? Except for the clear-cut case of a country still ruled by a legitimate government that requests help to repel an invasion, all other cases are subject to subtle distinctions. Who is asking me to intervene? A part of the citizenry? How representative of the country is this group, to what extent does intervention cloak, albeit with the noblest intentions, interference (Saguntium being a case in point)? Is intervention required when what happens in that country goes against our ethical principles? But are our principles the same as theirs? Is intervention necessary because for thousands of years a certain country has practiced ritual cannibalism, which is a horror for us but a religious practice there? Isn't this the way the white man shouldered his virtuous burden and subjected the peoples of civilizations that were ancient, although different from the white man's?

The only answer that strikes me as acceptable is that intervention is like a revolution. There is no previous law that says it is a good thing to do; on the contrary, revolutions are made despite laws and customs. The difference is that the decision to launch an international intervention springs not from a restricted elite or from an uncontrolled civil disturbance, but from talks among different peoples and governments. It is decided that although other people's opinions, customs, practices, and beliefs must be respected, something seems intolerable to us. Accepting the intolerable means casting doubt on our own identity. It is necessary to assume the responsibility of deciding what is intolerable and then taking action, ready to pay the price of error.

When an example of something wholly intolerable occurs, the threshold of intolerability is no longer the one fixed by the old laws. It is necessary to legislate anew. Of course, we have to be sure that the consensus regarding the new threshold of intolerability is as vast as possible, that it goes beyond national frontiers, and that it is in some way warranted by the "community"—a slippery concept, but one that underpins even the fact that we believe that the world turns. But then we need to choose.

What happened with Nazism and the Holocaust set a new threshold of intolerability. Over the centuries, there have been many cases of genocide, and in one way or another we have tolerated them all. We were weak, we were barbarians, we did not know what was happening more than ten miles away from our village. But this genocide was sanctioned (and carried into practice) in "scientific" terms, with an explicit request for consensus, even philosophical consensus, and propagandized as a planetary model. It did more than just violate our moral conscience: it threatened our philosophy and our science, our culture, our beliefs in good and evil. It attempted to wipe them out. We could not fail to respond to this threat. And the only possible response was to conclude that this would not be tolerable, not only immediately, but also fifty years after, and in the centuries to come.

It is in the contact of this level of intolerability that we find purulent the sordid bookkeeping of Holocaust deniers, who spend their time calculating whether the dead were really six million, as if five, four, two, or one million could provide grounds for some kind of a deal. And what if they were not gassed, but had died only because they had been left there without adequate care? Or if they died merely because of an allergic reaction to the tattoo?

But recognizing the intolerable means that all the accused at Nuremberg should have been condemned to hang even if only one person had died, and for simple failure to offer assistance at that. The new intolerable is not only genocide but its theorization. And this involves and places responsibility upon even the peons of slaughter. Faced with the intolerable, distinctions regarding intentions, good faith, and error all collapse: there is only objective responsibility. But (says one) I pushed the people into the gas chambers because they ordered me to do that, in reality I thought they were going to be deloused. That doesn't matter, I'm sorry, here we are dealing with the epiphany of the intolerable. The old laws with their mitigating circumstances don't count here: we shall sentence you to hang as well.

In order to assume this rule of conduct (a rule that also holds for the intolerable future, which obliges us to decide day by day where the intolerable lies), a society must be prepared to make many decisions, tough ones too, and to be united in shouldering all responsibilities. What disturbs us as an obscure element in the Priebke case is that it makes us aware that we are still a long way from taking this decision. That goes for young people and old alike, and not just Italians. Everyone has washed his hands of the problem: we have laws, let's leave this wretch to the courts.

Naturally today we might say that, after the Rome verdict, this joint capacity to define the intolerable is even farther off. But it was too far away even before the trial. And this is what continues to torment us—the (unconfessed) realization that we are jointly responsible.

So let's not ask ourselves for whom the bell tolls.

If you enjoyed reading *Five Moral Pieces*, look for these other titles by Umberto Eco

Baudolino
0-15-100690-3 / $27.00

The Name of the Rose
0-15-600131-4 (PB) / $15.00
0-15-144647-4 (HC) / $35.00

How to Travel with a Salmon & Other Essays
0-15-600125-X / $15.00

Misreadings
0-15-660752-2 / $14.00

Travels in Hyperreality
0-15-691321-6 / $15.00

Kant and the Platypus
0-15-601159-X / $16.00

Serendipities
0-15-600751-7 / $12.00

Foucault's Pendulum
0-15-132765-3 / $32.00

The Island of the Day Before
0-15-100151-0 / $25.00

CPSIA information can be obtained
at www.ICGtesting.com
Printed in the USA
FSHW011259060919
61784FS